"*On Love and Mercy* is a devotional that calls us to daily reflection around the understanding that justice work cannot be separated from one's faith and beliefs—that it truly is a vocation. In a time when we are so divided, it invites us to accept the truth that everyone is made in the image of God, and challenges us to love our neighbors as Jesus instructed us to. Living into these commandments can help heal our broken nation and world."

—**REV. JIM WALLIS**, inaugural holder of the Endowed Chair in Faith and Justice at the McCourt School of Public Policy, founding director of the Georgetown University Center on Faith and Justice, and founder of Sojourners

"*On Love and Mercy* is a devotional based on Jesus' most important instruction: to love our neighbors. Using Christ's life and words, Stephen Mattson's writing challenges us to do the work of social justice, and reminds us of its divine importance."

—**KAREN GONZÁLEZ**, immigration advocate and author of *The God Who Sees: Immigrants, the Bible, and the Journey to Belong*

"Stephen Mattson has been an important voice for social justice. His writing continues to inspire Christians to participate in the work of social justice. *On Love and Mercy* is faithfully rooted in the Scriptures and centers the words and life of Jesus Christ."

—**REV. DENNIS R. EDWARDS**, PhD, associate professor of New Testament at North Park Theological Seminary and author of *Might from the Margins: The Gospel's Power to Turn the Tables on Injustice*

"Stephen Mattson inspires us to love our neighbors by emulating Jesus and shows us that justice work is essential to faith."

—**BEN COHEN**, cofounder of Ben & Jerry's Ice Cream

"Stephen Mattson invites readers to read, hear, and live out the words of Jesus. He takes us on a journey through God's heart. This is a great devotional for those who may be straddling the fence in joining God to establish justice on earth."

—**REV. BRITTINI L. PALMER**, prophetic preacher, freedom writer, and communications consultant in Atlanta, Georgia

"Stephen Mattson writes with such openness and graciousness, inviting us all to consider social justice in our own lives. He has a way of making social justice and the connection to our faith accessible. Definitely get a copy and let it influence you the way it did me."

—CANDICE CZUBERNAT, founder of The Christian Closet

"*On Love and Mercy* helps redirect the many ways that Christianity has wielded power against the vulnerable to the justice teachings of Jesus."

—CINDY WANG BRANDT, author of *Parenting Forward: How to Raise Children with Justice, Mercy, and Kindness* and the children's book *You Are Revolutionary*

"*On Love and Mercy* is an inspiring devotional that challenges readers to expand their understanding and scope of what it means to engage in justice in the world. Deeply rooted in Scripture and yet deeply practical and connected to our modern world, Stephen Mattson has provided all who seek to embody love and mercy a powerful devotional to guide our reflection and nourish our souls."

—REV. BRANDAN ROBERTSON, author of the forthcoming *Filled to Be Emptied: The Path of Liberation for a Privileged People*

"*On Love and Mercy* does something unique: It thoughtfully describes a Christian theology of social justice in the format of meaningful, convicting, and prayerful daily devotions. The church needs more resources like this! Stephen Mattson has written an important book to help individuals, small groups, and church communities live just and faithful lives."

—KAITLYN SCHIESS, theologian and author of *The Liturgy of Politics: Spiritual Formation for the Sake of Our Neighbor*

"There have been many Christian books written about social justice but not many devotionals on this theme. This is why Stephen Mattson's *On Love and Mercy* is such a timely and powerful resource. As a Christian leader who has been involved in social justice for over thirty-five years, I can tell you that Mattson's devotional provides a much-needed anchor for our soul that will sustain us in the midst of the storms of social injustice present in our world today. I can't wait to order this book for all my team here at Connect City."

—REV. COLIN MCCARTNEY, founder of various urban-based nonprofits and codirector of Connect City (www.ConnectCity.org)

On Love & Mercy

A SOCIAL JUSTICE DEVOTIONAL

Stephen Mattson

Herald Press
PO Box 866, Harrisonburg, Virginia 22803
www.HeraldPress.com

Library of Congress Cataloging-in-Publication Data
Names: Mattson, Stephen, author.
Title: On love and mercy : a social justice devotional / Stephen Mattson.
Description: Harrisonburg, Virginia : Herald Press, 2021. | Includes bibliographical
    references.
Identifiers: LCCN 2021032839 (print) | LCCN 2021032840 (ebook) | ISBN
    9781513809373 (hardback) | ISBN 9781513809380 (ebook)
Subjects: LCSH: Christianity and justice—Prayers and devotions. | Social
    justice—Religious aspects—Christianity—Prayers and devotions. |
    Christian sociology—Prayers and devotions. | BISAC: RELIGION /
    Devotional | RELIGION / Christian Living / Devotional
Classification: LCC BR115.J8 M386 2021 (print) | LCC BR115.J8 (ebook) |
    DDC 261.8--dc23
LC record available at https://lccn.loc.gov/2021032839
LC ebook record available at https://lccn.loc.gov/2021032840

Study guides are available for many Herald Press titles at www.HeraldPress.com.

ON LOVE AND MERCY
© 2021 by Herald Press, Harrisonburg, Virginia 22803. 800-245-7894.
    All rights reserved.
Library of Congress Control Number: 2021032839
International Standard Book Number: 978-1-5138-0937-3 (hardcover)
    978-1-5138-0938-0 (ebook)
Printed in United States of America
Cover and interior design by Merrill Miller
Cover image by Janaka Maharage Dharmasena/ iStockphoto/Getty Images
Interior art by xochicalco/Getty Images

25 24 23 22 21   10 9 8 7 6 5 4 3 2 1

Contents

Removing the Stigma from Social Justice

THE TERM *SOCIAL JUSTICE* is loaded with political baggage. For some, it's a telltale sign of liberal agendas and heretical theology. But many others see social justice as a wonderful thing that in fact reflects the heart of Jesus. Theologian James Cone writes about the spiritual importance of incorporating social action in his critically acclaimed book *The Cross and the Lynching Tree*: "The gospel of Jesus is not a rational concept to be explained in a theory of salvation, but a story about God's presence in Jesus' solidarity with the oppressed, which led to his death on the cross. What is redemptive is the faith that God snatches victory out of defeat, life out of death, and hope out of despair."[1]

Social justice. A simple term loaded with explosive religious, political, and social implications. But the actual definitions of the word are quite disarming. With dictionary interpretations like "justice in terms of the distribution of wealth, opportunities, and privileges within a society"[2] and "a doctrine of egalitarianism"[3] (*egalitarianism* meaning a doctrine that all people are equal and deserve equal rights and opportunities) it's hard to imagine how anyone could be opposed to such causes. Yet the term continues to elicit strong emotions and divisions.

In the year 2018, a time filled with human catastrophes of epic proportions—a massive refugee crisis, monumental immigration movements, historic natural disasters, poverty, and numerous global wars and political movements, including police brutality, the #MeToo movement, and Black Lives Matter—it was the topic of social justice that inspired prominent Christian leaders (predominantly White and conservative) to draft, publish, and sign a major theological treatise entitled *The Statement on Social Justice and the Gospel*. The title itself hinted at what the content would suggest, and the corresponding website presented a theological outline warning that the concepts of "social justice" were in opposition to "the gospel."

This negative—even combative—attitude towards social justice among American Christians has grown in popularity among many mainstream Protestant faith communities. Renowned pastor and theologian John Piper once used the phrase "Hell is social justice" as part of a tweet,[4] and in an article entitled "Only Christians Understand True Social Justice" on his Desiring God website, author Bryce Young wrote:

> I live in a fairly progressive city. "Social justice" is precious cultural currency. Where you fall on any number of social issues can brand you a hero, a warrior, a victim, or a villain. And this isn't the case only in my city.
>
> Our culture as a whole is knee-deep in the mud pit fighting over the greased pig of "Justice": racial discrimination, abortion, welfare, healthcare, the environment, immigration, the definition of marriage, foreign policy, poverty rates, economic issues — what are your thoughts on . . . all of them? Where do you fall? Facebook feeds

and Twitter streams have become a social war zone with articles, op-eds, think pieces, and news updates as the ammunition fired between various ideologies.[5]

These two paragraphs summarize much of conservative Christianity's fear when it comes to social justice. First, the term is associated with progressivism—as if it's something New-Agey or liberal. For conservative White Christians, few things are worse than any form of political or theological liberalism. Next, the term social justice is wrapped in scare quotes, implying that it has some sort of malicious, hidden, or insincere intent behind it. Then the author relates social justice to being something owned and operated by "our culture," positioning the idea of social justice as something in conflict with orthodox Christianity, as if it's non-Christlike, secular, and primarily a cultural construct.

This kind of thinking has serious consequences. It dismisses justice issues like racial discrimination, immigration, poverty, foreign policy, economic inequality, incarceration rates, sexism, misogyny, xenophobia, and an array of vitally important topics that cut at the heart of who God is as "non-Christian" or props for some sort of political agenda—and therefore not worthy of "Christian" (meaning White, politically conservative Christian) support.

But the actual genesis of the term *social justice* offers a comforting origin story that is both politically neutral and spiritually hopeful. In an article for the Gospel Coalition, itself a politically conservative-leaning Evangelical organization, author Joe Carter noted that "Jesuit priest Luigi Taparelli D'Azeglio coined the term in the 1840s and based the concept on the teachings of Thomas Aquinas. Taparelli used the term to refer to the ordinary and traditional conception of justice applied to the constitutional arrangements of society. At the time, Taparelli's concept was considered a significant contribution to conservative political philosophy." Carter goes on to write, "It wasn't until the 1970s and the publication of John Rawls's *A Theory of Justice* that the term became widely associated with liberal secular political philosophy, particularly with changing social institutions."[6]

The Roman Catholic Church has long interpreted social justice as a distinctly holy endeavor. The Vatican even states within its own Catechism of the Catholic Church that "society ensures social justice when it provides the conditions that allow associations or individuals to obtain what is their due, according to their nature and their vocation. Social justice is linked to the common good and the exercise of authority," and, "Social justice can be obtained only in respecting the transcendent dignity of man. The person represents the ultimate end of society, which is ordered to him." This is followed immediately with a quote by Pope John Paul II: "What is at stake is the dignity of the human person, whose defense and promotion have been entrusted to us by the Creator, and to whom the men and women at every moment of history are strictly and responsibly in debt."[7]

Like many non-White and non-conservative Christians, the Catholic Church rightly views social justice as a holy Christian tradition. The pursuit of social justice is neither a partisan platform nor a secular cause, but rather a righteous endeavor exemplified perfectly by the person of Jesus.

Within Christianity, the contradicting views on what social justice actually is, and what it means, can create a lot of confusion and misunderstanding. But if we take the words *social* and *justice* and look at their distinct meanings, we can get a clearer idea of what *social justice* might actually mean.

By definition, the word *social* means "relating to society or its organization."[8] The word *justice* means "the quality of being just, impartial, or fair."[9] Simply put, and for the purpose of this devotional, the definition we'll use for the term *social justice* is simply this: *justice within a society.*

From this foundation of wanting, pursuing, and implementing *justice within our society*, we can confidently as Christ-followers know that social justice is indeed a godly venture. May we "learn to do good; seek justice, correct oppression; bring justice to the fatherless, plead the widow's cause" (Isaiah 1:17 ESV).

As Christ has shown us through his life and words, the best way to bring about social justice in a society is through love. To love others is what social justice work is all about, and it's also what Jesus commanded us to do. Christianity and social justice go hand in hand, and we can be confident in our pursuit of implementing justice within our society because in doing so we're being like Jesus.

DAY 1

Social Justice Is Holy

But let justice roll down like waters, and righteousness like an ever-flowing stream. —**AMOS 5:24**

When justice is done, it is a joy to the righteous but terror to evildoers. —**PROVERBS 21:15**

Learn to do good; seek justice, correct oppression; bring justice to the fatherless, plead the widow's cause. —**ISAIAH 1:17**

He has told you, O man, what is good; and what does the Lord require of you but to do justice, and to love kindness, and to walk humbly with your God? —**MICAH 6:8**

Therefore the Lord waits to be gracious to you, and therefore he exalts himself to show mercy to you. For the Lord is a God of justice; blessed are all those who wait for him. —**ISAIAH 30:18**

SOCIAL JUSTICE—justice within our society—is a holy and godly pursuit. If you're trying to follow Jesus, you can find comfort in knowing that pursuing social justice is a Christlike discipline that emulates the words, actions, and commands of Christ. It will help you understand Jesus in a deep and personal way. We're inspired to advance social justice because it's what Jesus did and what he's doing right now—through *us*. The divine power of Christ's Spirit gives us a passion for justice, and if this passion is waning or nonexistent within you, pray that the Holy Spirit renews this conviction so that your soul will be a light within the darkness. Because social justice *is* a light within our world, a form of righteousness meant to shine upon a hill, glorifying God through the good works done for the love of others.

Do not be fooled. Social justice isn't a political agenda, popular fad, or mere hobby for the discontented. It's not a secular construct or misguided venture. Instead, social justice is one of the holiest Christian traditions, where followers of Jesus are tasked with honoring, protecting, and loving humanity. Social justice helps the oppressed, liberates the entrapped, and embodies love, mercy, and peace within our world. It takes many forms, bringing care and healing to the sick, financial stability to the poor, punishment to the criminal, justice to the victim, citizenship to the alien, restitution to the wronged, food and shelter to the destitute, freedom to the enslaved, and love to our neighbors. Social justice is a journey towards God, a holy pilgrimage that can only be done through acts of loving humanity. And each day is an opportunity to progress towards God, towards loving others, towards justice.

MEDITATION

Do you consider social justice to be a Christian tradition? How did Jesus and other people in the Bible pursue social justice within their world?

PRAYER

God of love and mercy, God of justice, please use my life to bring love and mercy and justice to the world around me. May I be a light within the darkness. During times of personal struggle or outside hostility, remind me of the holy importance of social justice and renew my passion for loving others.

DAY 2

The Importance of Social Justice

When justice is done, it is a joy to the righteous but terror to evildoers. —**PROVERBS 21:15**

SOCIAL JUSTICE is a righteous cause and a holy endeavor. It isn't a hobby or minor theological concept—it's a matter of life and death. Trivializing its importance risks the very lives of those being oppressed. To dismiss social justice is to dismiss the worth and humanity of your neighbor.

There will be those who denounce it, co-opt it, minimize its importance, and hate it. To commit yourself to social justice is to commit yourself to being the target of hate, slander, and abuse. You may sometimes feel abandoned, but God is on your side: "Thus says the LORD: Do justice and righteousness, and deliver from the hand of the oppressor him who has been robbed. And do no wrong or violence to the resident alien, the fatherless, and the widow, nor shed innocent blood in this place" (Jeremiah 22:3).

To pursue social justice is to participate in goodness and resist those who oppress. It's choosing a side in the supernatural battle of good vs. evil, where the stakes are the real lives of our friends, relatives, neighbors, and the countless people that are experiencing various forms of injustice all around us. Prepare yourself, then go forth and engage in today's clash with injustice knowing that God is on your side.

MEDITATION

How important is social justice to your Christian faith? Do you believe in a supernatural conflict that impacts the material world around us?

> For we do not wrestle against flesh and blood, but against the rulers, against the authorities, against the cosmic powers over this present darkness, against the spiritual forces of evil in the heavenly places. —**EPHESIANS 6:12**

PRAYER

God, you are "our refuge and strength, a very present help in trouble." Therefore I "will not fear though the earth gives way, though the mountains be moved into the heart of the sea, though its waters roar and foam, though the mountains tremble at its swelling" (Psalm 46:1-3). I will not fear the evils of injustice or be scared of those who commit them.

God, you are "my refuge and my fortress, my God, in whom I trust" (Psalm 91:2-6). Thank you for being on the side of justice, for taking up the cause of the oppressed, and for defending the victim. Be my strength, and help me to remember that "they who wait for the LORD shall renew their strength; they shall mount up with wings like eagles; they shall run and not be weary; they shall walk and not faint" (Isaiah 40:31). Renew my determination, God. Take up the cause of the oppressed. May I rise up. May I resist the wicked. May I follow you, God of truth and justice and love.

The Greatest Commandments: Love God and Love Your Neighbor

"Teacher, which is the great commandment in the Law?" And he said to him, "You shall love the Lord your God with all your heart and with all your soul and with all your mind. This is the great and first commandment. And a second is like it: You shall love your neighbor as yourself. On these two commandments depend all the Law and the Prophets." —**MATTHEW 22:36-40**

THE EXAMPLE OF JESUS shows us how to right wrongs, seek and defend truth, and love the maligned and outcast as our very own. For those who believe in the hope and power of Jesus, social justice is a uniquely Christian tradition personified by Christ himself. Christianity, then, *should* be a wonderful conduit of social justice.

But, just like the term *social justice*, Christianity means many different things to many different people. For some it's defined by voting for a certain political party, holding a specific moral belief, or attending church on Sundays. For others it requires being part of a particular denomination or adhering to defined theological doctrines. In this complex world, the term *Christian* can conjure up acts of charity and goodwill or of violence and hate. Being labeled a Christian can be interpreted as either an insult or a compliment, and both would be justifiable.

Christianity manifests itself differently in various forms. Christianity can be Protestant, Catholic, or Orthodox. It can be American, Iraqi, Russian, Chinese, Ethiopian, or any nationality, ethnicity, culture, or language. Christians can be any age, and can identify as any gender. Christians can be liberal or conservative, Republican or Democrat or socialist, even anarchist. Christian personalities can be good or bad, heroes or villains, and are oftentimes both. What it means to be a Christian can be perceived and explained in infinitely different—and often contradictory—ways. This is why we begin here, with these verses.

Because Jesus is being asked: What is the point of it all? What *is* Christianity? And this is his answer: to "love the Lord your God with all your heart and with all your soul and with all your mind" and "love your neighbor as yourself." Like Christianity itself, this is also the very foundation of social justice: to love your neighbor as yourself.

MEDITATION

In your opinion, what *is* the point of it all? What is Christianity? Have you ever asked yourself what Christianity even is, or who it's for, or what the goal of it is? Take some time to ponder these monumental questions.

PRAYER

Dear God, I love you with all my heart and soul and mind. God, thank you for loving me, and thank you for loving my neighbors. Please help me to love my neighbors to the best of my ability, with the same passion and love that you show them.

Who Is Your Neighbor?

And behold, a lawyer stood up to put him to the test, saying, "Teacher, what shall I do to inherit eternal life?" He said to him, "What is written in the Law? How do you read it?" And he answered, "You shall love the Lord your God with all your heart and with all your soul and with all your strength and with all your mind, and your neighbor as yourself." And he said to him, "You have answered correctly; do this, and you will live."

But he, desiring to justify himself, said to Jesus, "And who is my neighbor?" Jesus replied, "A man was going down from Jerusalem to Jericho, and he fell among robbers, who stripped him and beat him and departed, leaving him half dead. Now by chance a priest was going down that road, and when he saw him he passed by on the other side. So likewise a Levite, when he came to the place and saw him, passed by on the other side. But a Samaritan, as he journeyed, came to where he was, and when he saw him, he had compassion. He went to him and bound up his wounds, pouring on oil and wine. Then he set him on his own animal and brought him to an inn and took care of him. And the next day he took out two denarii and gave them to the innkeeper, saying, 'Take care of him, and whatever more you spend, I will repay you when I come back.' Which of these three, do you think, proved to be a neighbor to the man who fell among the robbers?" He said, "The one who showed him mercy." And Jesus said to him, "You go, and do likewise." —**LUKE 10:25-37**

IF FOLLOWING CHRIST and pursuing social justice means loving our neighbors, it begs the very question asked by the lawyer: "And who is my neighbor?"

Jesus responds by telling the parable of the good Samaritan. This isn't merely a story about a virtuous stranger doing a good deed; it's a radical and provocative lesson that many during that time would have considered religious and societal heresy. The Jewish audience listening to Jesus would have been shocked by who he cast as the righteous and the unrighteous. Due to various political, religious, and cultural differences and conflicts, the Samaritans were hated and despised. Violence—even war—erupted between these factions, and they regularly killed each other.

To frame a Samaritan as doing the right thing—loving his neighbor and therefore emulating a Jesus-following life—would be almost unfathomable. If this exact same parable would be retold in today's modern era, it would be as if a Zionist Israeli citizen were mugged, and while both a Jewish rabbi and Israeli soldier passed by and did nothing, a Palestinian member of Hamas stopped and was "the good Samaritan" who immediately helped the Zionist and cared for him, and then paid for his medical expenses. For Zionist Israelis living in conflict with Hamas—and for Hamas members—this story would be scandalous.

But much of following Jesus feels scandalous. Jesus challenges us to love our "neighbor," which includes those who don't share—and who may even be in opposition to—our political, religious, social, ethnic, and cultural identities. Likewise, through this story Jesus challenges us to rethink who we consider "good" and "bad." We may have grown up to believe that the police, army, and government were inherently good—but what if our heroes are actually the ones committing injustice, are complicit participants, or at the very least are apathetic to the plight of others?

Christians professing to follow Jesus have widely accepted the mantra to love God—the first part of Jesus's "greatest command." But continuing on to the second, fewer fully understand or live out what it means to love their neighbor. Because as the lawyer who posed the question learned, a neighbor isn't just someone who lives next to us, or who shares our ideological and religious worldview. Our neighbor is *everyone,* even those we consider "bad" or "unworthy."

Social justice—like Jesus—is inclusive, even to our very worst enemies. Favoritism, bias, and exceptionalism contradict its very essence and are strong signs and symptoms of *injustice.* By its very nature, justice cannot be partial. Social justice can never make exceptions towards others based on their religion, culture, political beliefs, race, ethnicity, skin color, gender, nationality, or any difference, great or small. God invites us to embrace others with an all-encompassing love.

MEDITATION

Has your church, faith community, or upbringing overtly taught or insinuated that a particular person, people group, or affiliation is "less-than" or unworthy of love?

Within your social networks and communities, which people groups or individuals are typically considered "good" and "bad?" How have these perceptions impacted the way they are treated? How has your faith tradition either validated or invalidated these assumptions?

PRAYER

God, please help me to start seeing the best in people and to realize that my assumptions about who is good and who is bad are wrong. Help me to love my neighbors—all of them.

DAY 5

Love Your Enemy

"You have heard that it was said, 'Love your neighbor and hate your enemy.' But I tell you, love your enemies and pray for those who persecute you, that you may be children of your Father in heaven."

—MATTHEW 5:43-45 NIV

AS IF TO CLEAR UP any possible confusion about who God calls us to love, in this passage Jesus goes beyond the term *neighbor* to include enemies: *"Love your enemies . . ."*

For those committed to following Jesus, any political, social, or religious controversy can be approached by asking ourselves: *What is the most loving action or response?*

And yet much of our Christian culture forsakes this gospel of Christ for a narrative of fear, hate, and judgment—demonizing others for financial, political, or relational support. We wage culture wars as us ("righteous Christians") vs. them (our "enemies"). Christians even like to attack other Christians for having the "wrong" beliefs or adhering to the "wrong" practices. Under the guise of truth, doctrine, and holiness, we can unfairly label others as being sinful, dangerous, and our enemy.

This ignores the greatest truth: that God is love, and that by loving our enemies as ourselves we are following God's example. Any Christian movement, action, or message that prevents, diminishes, or opposes being loving towards others—even our enemies—is a form of idolatry.

We see this co-opting of Christianity when politicians and partisan platforms vie for Christian votes and support by weaponizing morality to pit one group of people against another. But vilifying anyone, whether they're immigrants, undocumented immigrants, refugees, the homeless, foreigners, atheists, or whoever else might get labeled as "the other" misses the mark of God's love. To be loving towards others, whether they're our neighbors or our enemies, is a wonderful example of emulating Jesus and fulfilling his greatest command.

Loving your enemy doesn't mean dismissing wrongdoings or diminishing hurtful words or actions, and it doesn't mean you stop protecting yourself and others from forms of abuse, pain, or violence. Wrongdoers still face the consequences of their actions. "Loving your enemy" doesn't mean preventing legal action, or halting the pursuit of justice and truth. It's important to understand that love should never be a concept or practice that enables or participates in oppression in any way.

Can you imagine not having a single enemy—no work enemies, school enemies, or political enemies? It's hard to envision this within our broken world, but this is how God sees humanity. *Every* person is divinely loved by God, as if they are God's own children.

Social justice reminds Christians that Christlike love is our ultimate purpose. Perhaps no Christian discipline depends more wholly and completely on embracing the sacrificial and selfless love of Christ.

MEDITATION

Who do you consider your enemy? Who are your political, social, national, and religious enemies? Have you ever considered how to love them? In what ways can you practice the Christlike discipline of loving them?

PRAYER

Dear God, help me to love my enemies, to humanize them, to admit that they are divinely and passionately loved by you. To hate them is to hate a divinely created person made in your image. Help me not to deny truth, give me the courage to protect myself and others, and remind me that love should never enable abuse or empower an abuser. Thank you for valuing my physical, emotional, and mental well-being, and my safety. Forgive me for hating my enemies, and help me to forgive them just as you have forgiven me. I ask for the strength to love them.

No, Seriously! Love Your Enemy!

But I say to you who hear, Love your enemies, do good to those who
hate you, bless those who curse you, pray for those who abuse you.
To one who strikes you on the cheek, offer the other also, and from
one who takes away your cloak do not withhold your tunic either.
Give to everyone who begs from you, and from one who takes away
your goods do not demand them back. And as you wish that others
would do to you, do so to them.

—LUKE 6:27-31

MAYBE NO COMMAND is harder for Christians to accept or follow than Christ's instruction to love our enemies. It's only natural to
want to avoid them, and to return hate with hate. Yet Jesus tells us
more than once to love them!

To love our enemies is to accept and embody the divine truth that
everyone is created in God's image and loved by God. Enemy-love
trusts in the existence of redemption and puts faith and hope in God's
ability to change someone's heart and mind. This hope for transfor-
mation relies on the impetus of love, not hate or violence or death. It

bestows the same grace and mercy and love and justice on others that God has shown to us.

Loving our enemy doesn't negate the consequences of an enemy's actions or downplay the seriousness of oppression or injustice. And God's unconditional love does not mean an unconditional acceptance of one's complicity with oppression or injustice. It's not the absence of justice or even the existence of friendship. To love our enemies doesn't mean we have to compromise our convictions, or in any way accept their oppression or wrongdoings. It's not conceding or letting them have a free pass. Loving our enemy still requires truth-telling, calling on them do what's right (for their sake and ours), having them make amends and face the reality of their choices.

It's also important to create healthy boundaries for ourselves. That may or may not mean having any sort of relationship with our enemy, but God asks that we treat others with human dignity, not with hate or violence. To love our enemy is to embrace the power of love and goodness even within the midst of experiencing hate, oppression, and injustice from someone else.

Even as we begin to understand the theology of enemy love, its practical applications are extraordinarily difficult and nearly impossible to do without God's supernatural help. The psalmist cries out to God with frustration, venting about the difficulty of trying to love their enemies: "Be not silent, O God of my praise! For wicked and deceitful mouths are opened against me, speaking against me with lying tongues. They encircle me with words of hate, and attack me without cause. In return for my love they accuse me, but I give myself to prayer. So they reward me evil for good, and hatred for my love" (Psalm 109:1-5). This is why we must invite the Holy Spirit into the difficult work of social justice, especially when facing people who refuse to stop oppressing, who continue to hurt, hate, and attack.

How our enemy reacts to our love isn't our responsibility. God doesn't demand that we force our enemy to change or transform (although it could happen), but God does request that we take our charge of loving others seriously, no matter how they react. The psalmist realizes this and declares that God will take on the burden of dealing with their enemies:

> Help me, O LORD my God!
>> Save me according to your steadfast love!
> Let them know that this is your hand;
>> you, O LORD, have done it!
> Let them curse, but you will bless!
>> They arise and are put to shame, but your servant will be glad!
> May my accusers be clothed with dishonor;
>> may they be wrapped in their own shame as in a cloak!
>
> With my mouth I will give great thanks to the LORD:
>> I will praise him in the midst of the throng.
> For he stands at the right hand of the needy one,
>> to save him from those who condemn his soul to death.
>
> **—PSALM 109:26-31**

Social justice has lots of enemies, but God isn't one of them. If we cannot love our enemies, we'll quickly become exhausted. The emotional, mental, physical, and spiritual energy it takes to fuel animosity and hostility towards others is unsustainable and will always cause more harm than good. Only the divine love of God can handle the enormous task of engaging with our enemies to overcome oppression and injustice.

MEDITATION

Can you think of any example of someone who chose to love their enemy? What do you think loving your enemy is or isn't? Can it ever be wrong or unhealthy to love your enemy? Why or why not?

> Fret not yourself because of evildoers;
> > be not envious of wrongdoers!
> For they will soon fade like the grass
> > and wither like the green herb.
>
> Trust in the LORD, and do good;
> > dwell in the land and befriend faithfulness.
> Delight yourself in the LORD,
> > and he will give you the desires of your heart.
>
> Commit your way to the LORD;
> > trust in him, and he will act.

—PSALM 37:1-5

PRAYER

Dear God, again I earnestly pray that I will love my enemies instead of fear them. Be my source of hope and strength. Let me put my confidence in you. Prince of Peace, make me a peacemaker, someone who heals relationships instead of breaks them. May my life be a testament of your love, where I work to build communities that are formed through neighborly friendships.

DAY 7

⟵

Follow Jesus

"And Jesus came and said to them, 'All authority in heaven and on earth has been given to me. Go therefore and make disciples of all nations, baptizing them in the name of the Father and of the Son and of the Holy Spirit, teaching them to observe all that I have commanded you.'" —**MATTHEW 28:18-20**

THE GREAT COMMISSION is regarded as Christianity's most important mandate for evangelism, yet many skim over these verses without really understanding Christ's astounding claim: "*All authority in heaven and on earth has been given to me.*" The "me" in these verses is Jesus, and he's making a bold statement of his own divinity. These verses are extraordinary not only because they reveal who has received this supreme, divine authority—Jesus—but also because of who is excluded. This divine authority, which constitutes what is right and wrong, good and evil, and the embodiment of godly holiness, has *not* been given exclusively to the church, the American government, or the pastor of your church. Rather, it has been given to Jesus.

But how often have we treated our church, our theological beliefs, or even ourselves as the ultimate authority? Unfortunately, too often. But Jesus is saying that only he can claim this honor. This is why the thoughts, words, and actions of social justice should always be framed around the thoughts, words, and actions of Jesus.

Sadly, Christianity can sometimes become everything but Christlike. Instead of seeing Christianity as a manifestation of Jesus' love of God and humanity, many have used military might to force their beliefs on those they have conquered. Others have tried using money, wealth, and materialism to manipulate the oppressed into an acceptance of Christianity or a forced subservience to its rulers in order to avoid further punishment. We've also used laws, courts, and judicial systems to legislate our preferred brand of religious practice into legal mandates for entire populations. We've worked within political systems to lobby for religious power and control, and entire empires have been built under the premise of expanding Christianity to the world. Many have accomplished this through violence, forcefully bringing "Christianity" through the sword, under the threat of death, torture, and violent oppression. But time and again, all of these methods have utterly failed to manifest the love of Jesus and done way more harm than good, rather than reflecting the beautifully divine and good nature of God.

To prioritize our neighbors above money, safety, comfort, and power is to observe what Christ commanded and thus fulfill the great commission. Social justice is a holy endeavor, one of the very first commands of the early church, originating from the words and actions of Jesus himself.

MEDITATION

Social justice is founded upon selflessly loving others. How have your experiences within Christianity (as distinct from following Jesus) inhibited your ability to love God and love others? How have they set a good example?

Identify an aspect of Christianity—a doctrine, denominational practice, belief—that is detrimental to loving God and loving others, and then mentally commit to discarding it.

PRAYER

God, help me to see where my religious beliefs or faith practice need to align with loving my neighbor. I pray that my Christianity will never prevent me from being Christlike. Forgive me for the times I've withheld love, and even hated others, because of my religion. Thank you for your ceaseless love.

DAY 8

The Bible, Jesus, and Justice

In the beginning was the Word, and the Word was with God, and the Word was God. He was in the beginning with God. All things were made through him, and without him was not any thing made that was made. In him was life, and the life was the light of men. The light shines in the darkness, and the darkness has not overcome it. —JOHN 1:1-5

SINCE CHRIST IS OUR ultimate example of how to pursue social justice, studying his life and words by reading Scripture is a wise endeavor. Christianity's holy book is the Bible, and so we must take the time to reflect upon a very important question: *What's the purpose of this book?* This is an important question, because the Bible has been used for all sorts of holy and unholy endeavors. In order to answer that question, we must first consider how we got this book in the first place.

As Christians, we can mostly think of the Bible in spiritual terms, as a Holy Spirit–inspired divine revelation—a holy message from God. And it is this. "All Scripture is God-breathed and is useful for teaching, rebuking, correcting and training in righteousness, so that the servant of God may be thoroughly equipped for every good work" (2 Timothy 3:16-17 NIV). But in practical terms, the Bible is also a compilation of texts written by numerous authors who came from diverse social, religious, cultural, economic, and political backgrounds, who used different ancient languages, who wrote in diverse genres, who implemented unique styles, and who communicated to several distinct audiences spanning hundreds of years of history.

Then these writings were distributed, copied, and redistributed over and over again to many different people at many different places and times, only to be rediscovered years later, sometimes centuries later, at even more differing places and times. People documented, collected, and interpreted these writings, various religious councils debated and voted on them, and only then were they compiled into what we now call "the Bible."

But new discoveries were continually being made, such as newly-found manuscripts and the ability to cross-reference previously unshared materials. This required textual adjustments that in turn produced new interpretations and debates of what should be included in "the Bible," and what various words and passages mean or don't mean. This led to countless translations, written in various new languages and dialects, which were then copied and redistributed to the masses. To this day, new translations interpreting what the original texts actually meant continue to be published, and matters related to textual meaning, inclusion, accuracy, and inerrancy are a source of many questions and discussion.

In some sense, the creation of what we call the Bible is a never-ending process. We have an example of its diversity at our very fingertips: try going to a website that offers multiple versions of the Bible and look up the passage of Matthew 22:36-40. Now go to the dropdown menu that offers different versions of the Bible (NIV, ESV, KJV, etc.) and scroll through it. There are probably dozens of translations to choose from, with various language options, but even here the list is severely limited, and it doesn't come close to the estimated seven hundred languages into which the Bible has been translated.

All this brings us the Bible as we have it today—a divinely inspired collection of books with a major unifying theme: Jesus.

From beginning to end, the Bible points its readers to the person of Christ. Prophesied about in the Old Testament and documented in detail throughout the gospels of Matthew, Mark, Luke, and John, and the rest of the New Testament, in the person of Jesus we see exactly who God incarnate was and is.

If we believe that the ultimate purpose of the Bible is to point its readers to the glory of Jesus, and if we believe the declaration in Hebrews 1:3 that Jesus "is the radiance of the glory of God and the exact imprint of his nature, and he upholds the universe by the word of his power," then it makes sense to seek Jesus as an example to follow. When Jesus clearly and boldly declares what he considers the most important things in life—to love God and love our neighbors—he offers us a path we can follow. Christianity is about Christ, and over and over again his words and actions show us that to love our neighbor as ourself—to bring about social justice—is a noble pursuit.

MEDITATION

What do you think is the purpose of the Bible? In one or two sentences, can you describe why God "breathed" the Bible (in Timothy's words)? How did Jesus manifest social justice to the world around Him?

PRAYER

God, may I see your message as a story pointing to the love of Jesus. I want to use the Bible as a tool of love, to love you more, and to love my neighbors more. Forgive me for the times I use it to hate and to hurt. Help me never to lose sight of the person the Bible is pointing me to: you.

DAY 9

Jesus is God

Now when Jesus came into the district of Caesarea Philippi, he
asked his disciples, "Who do people say that the Son of Man is?"
And they said, "Some say John the Baptist, others say Elijah, and
others Jeremiah or one of the prophets." He said to them, "But who
do you say that I am?" —**MATTHEW 16:13-15**

SINCE CHRISTIANITY—and social justice—is ultimately about
pursuing Christ, it's good to understand that Jesus is not only God, but
he's also a gracious, merciful, peaceful, just, and loving God.

Every single human is unique, and each of us exists within a distinct
time and place. Right now, within the entire known universe, you're
the only person reading this exact sentence within this exact moment,
in your exact location, with whatever exact bodily position, mental
capacity, and feeling you currently have. However mundane reading
the previous sentence was, your experience of it was also extraordinarily
one-of-a-kind. Our existence is distinctly shaped by our specific environments, physicality, bodies, actions, expressions, experiences, and

relationships, which we in turn process and try to understand through our particular senses, emotions, thoughts, awareness, spirituality, and instincts.

It is a beautiful and magnificent truth that, across almost two thousand years, billions of us utterly uncommon, peculiar, and unfamiliar individuals have somehow all managed to love and follow a common individual: Jesus.

And yet it's also true that our perception of Jesus is influenced by the infinite factors that make up our particular existence: our friends, families, communities, cultures, beliefs, and societies all alter the way we understand, worship, and *see* Jesus.

Social justice work helps us to see things as they really are, and this gives us the humility to know our own biases and limitations. Through God's grace we can work hard to identify and avoid ignorance, apathy, and complicity. Social justice work also requests that we're honest, braver, and maintain a strong mind. In order to do this, God invites us to center our lives upon Jesus.

Over the last hundreds of years there have been massive migratory movements of people, cultural and industrial revolutions, and technological advances that continually seem to outpace our capacity to adapt to them. The world is in many ways radically different since the time of Christ, and it's easy for us to be blind to the ways that our understanding of the person of Jesus is shaped and manipulated according to our own cultural prejudices, modern perceptions, and societal expectations. Yet, he still asks of us, "But who do you say that I am?"

Our answer to that question, over all time, serves as our constant hope and inspiration: Jesus is God.

This is the answer Peter gave to Jesus when asked. But Peter's later actions signaled that Jesus probably wasn't the type of God he had hoped for or expected. Peter, who would later deny Christ three times, may have desired the kind of God who would use overwhelming military force and political power in order to establish a kingdom. It wouldn't be unreasonable for Peter to think like this; this was what being a god—an emperor—looked like in his culture, living under the rule and authority of a rich and powerful Roman empire.

Believing in God is one thing, but seeing the true identity of God is quite another.

Jesus is God. But Jesus was also an Aramaic-speaking Middle Eastern man. Jesus was Jewish, an ethnic minority. Jesus was a refugee. Jesus was an immigrant. Jesus was a criminal who was tried according to the Roman legal system and found guilty. Jesus was given the death penalty. Jesus was—and still is—all of those things. *This* is who we worship as our Lord and Savior.

Jesus never was, still isn't, and never will be a White American. He's not a Baptist, Catholic, or Greek Orthodox. He's not a Republican or a Democrat.

It's easy to transform God into the image of our own idols: wealth, power, and control. We can create our own version of God who likes, hates, and values the same things—and people—we do. But today, try to envision Jesus without all of the personal, cultural, and societal trappings we've bestowed upon him. Envision Jesus as a man with olive-brown skin, the Middle Eastern Jewish minority, immigrant, refugee, and convicted criminal the Bible reveals him to be.

The more we can acknowledge the social biases that influence our image of God, the better we'll be able to strip them away and see who God truly is.

MEDITATION

Have you ever acknowledged God as Middle Eastern, an ethnic minority, immigrant, refugee, and convicted criminal? What does it mean to you to worship this kind of God?

In what ways has your unique upbringing and your one-of-a-kind existence within the world shaped your view of God? How have different relationships or experiences changed the way you see God?

PRAYER

Jesus, may I always remember that you are "the image of the invisible God, the firstborn of all creation. For by him all things were created, in heaven and on earth, visible and invisible, whether thrones or dominions or rulers or authorities—all things were created through him and for him. And he is before all things, and in him all things hold together. And he is the head of the body, the church. He is the beginning, the firstborn from the dead, that in everything he might be preeminent. For in him all the fullness of God was pleased to dwell, and through him to reconcile to himself all things, whether on earth or in heaven, making peace by the blood of his cross" (Colossians 1:15-20).

Dear Jesus, help me to see you as a Middle Eastern ethnic minority, an immigrant, a refugee, and a criminal. May this understanding help me to love my neighbor as myself, and realize that your kingdom isn't manifested through political maneuvering or martial strength, but through the holy and sacrificial work of love, joy, peace, kindness, and justice.

Love

If I speak in the tongues of men and of angels, but have not love, I am a noisy gong or a clanging cymbal. And if I have prophetic powers, and understand all mysteries and all knowledge, and if I have all faith, so as to remove mountains, but have not love, I am nothing. If I give away all I have, and if I deliver up my body to be burned, but have not love, I gain nothing.

Love is patient and kind; love does not envy or boast; it is not arrogant or rude. It does not insist on its own way; it is not irritable or resentful; it does not rejoice at wrongdoing, but rejoices with the truth. Love bears all things, believes all things, hopes all things, endures all things.

Love never ends. As for prophecies, they will pass away; as for tongues, they will cease; as for knowledge, it will pass away. For we know in part and we prophesy in part, but when the perfect comes, the partial will pass away. When I was a child, I spoke like a child, I thought like a child, I reasoned like a child. When I became a man, I gave up childish ways. For now we see in a mirror dimly, but then face to face. Now I know in part; then I shall know fully, even as I have been fully known.

So now faith, hope, and love abide, these three; but the
greatest of these is love. —**1 CORINTHIANS 13:1-13**

WHILE SOME will try to co-opt, gaslight, manipulate, discredit, and
blame social justice—and the people who pursue it—for all types of
wrongdoing, mistakes, and agendas, these verses show us the transfor-
mational power of loving our neighbors as ourselves. The work of social
justice is practically applying the principle of loving your neighbor. It's
not a coincidence that acts of love towards others, and pursuing justice
and mercy for the oppressed, are also the exact beliefs and practices of
Jesus. Without this love, you gain nothing. With it, you have everything. The message of the gospel is the message of social justice: love is
everything.

This Christlike love is simple to understand yet difficult to consistently practice. It challenges us to be sacrificial, humble, and loving. So
difficult is this work that it's tempting for us to spend lifetimes building
financial empires and professional careers and devoting ourselves to rig-
orous spiritual practices instead of loving our neighbors, because these
all seem like easier options than the one Jesus calls us to.

To pursue Jesus is to love the world around us. God makes appeals
to us to have love-based attitudes and actions towards the poor, sick,
incarcerated, detained, homeless, hungry, deported, abused, and
oppressed. To love these neighbors of ours is the Jesus way.

Unfortunately, love isn't the primary motivation for the systems
and institutions around us. They are built to pursue power and wealth
above all else. For these entities—corporations, governments, and
sometimes even religious communities—the way of Christ is often
perceived as being illogical, inefficient, unfair, and even absurd. It has
no interest in pursuing what they value most. When success is based
upon the amount of financial wealth, popularity, power, and control
one possesses, love becomes of little use and value.

When we value this kind of superficial prosperity above all else, all other values—even morality, truth, and character—become subservient to that quest. This idolization of wealth and power skews the way religion, entertainment, work, politics, and even justice operate in our world. Dehumanization and oppression thrive because love is a worthless commodity within an economy that runs on money, power, and fame.

Power, fame, and money *can* be utilized to pursue social justice, but should *never* be used if love—the inspiration, goal, and outcome of social justice—is compromised even in the slightest. Because while love is useless to the profit-driven machinations that fuel power-hungry societies, it is the very lifeblood of social justice.

Pursuits of wealth, power, and fame are often primary sources of oppression because they rely on theft, exploitation, greed, dishonesty, and injustice. The only reliable and consistent force that has ever successfully overcome injustice is the pursuit of love, which has always been the primary source of hope and freedom. As followers of Christ, God urges us to treat our neighbors, and even our enemies, with this wondrous love.

Where do we start, and how do we become people who love? Let's look to the person of Jesus as the perfect example. When we do this, we realize that his life, words, and actions were less about saying the right things or belonging to religious institutions and more about practically loving all people and bringing them justice, peace, kindness, hope, and truth. Jesus' life focused on bearing the burdens and ending the sufferings of others—social justice. May we go and do likewise.

MEDITATION

In what ways do we overvalue money and undervalue love? How does our society influence and shape the way we view things as being valuable? How does it shape people as being either valuable or invaluable?

PRAYER

God, give me a heart that would rather I be loving than rich, powerful, or famous. Forgive me for the ways I've attempted to compensate for not loving others. Help me to remember that donating money, adhering to spiritual beliefs, attending religious services, studying theological doctrines, and passionately proclaiming Christian rhetoric is all worthless, a noisy gong, if it lacks love. Give me the strength to love.

DAY 11

Citizenship

But our citizenship is in heaven, and from it we await a Savior, the
Lord Jesus Christ. —**PHILIPPIANS 3:20**

FOLLOWING CHRIST implores us to pledge allegiance to Jesus
above any earthly king, leader, political party, or government. A
Christian is a citizen of the kingdom of God, and this royal priesthood
supersedes any other citizenship.

The discipline of pursuing social justice exemplifies the spirit of
devotion to Jesus and Christ's kingdom more than almost any other
spiritual practice, because it serves, honors, and loves those whom the
governments of earth have discarded, oppressed, and hated.

Citizenship of a nation usually offers certain rights and services,
which can include forms of welfare, safety, legal protection, and community. But it can also lead to nationalism, xenophobia, colonialism,
violence, and war. Governments—along with their political parties,
politicians, armies, laws, and policies—will often be anti-Christian in

nature, greedily pursuing wealth, power, and influence no matter the cost, for the benefit of themselves and at the expense of others. This happens because countries don't have the same goal—to sacrificially love others—as the kingdom of God.

Citizenship in the kingdom of God is different. The kingdom of God values love above everything. Its citizens follow Jesus as their ruler and strive to emulate his life through word and deed. The power of God's kingdom is established through sacrificial love. It prioritizes others above oneself. Following Jesus often contradicts the actions and agendas of your country, government, and preferred political party. It's important to recognize and honor your divine loyalty to the kingdom of God above any other authority—every day you will be faced with decisions that could pull you in either direction, and it's often easier to succumb to your earthly citizenship than to follow Christ.

Being a dutiful citizen of your state is a common excuse to avoid pursuing both Jesus and social justice, because it can be a pathway to benefit yourself while simultaneously harming your neighbor. For example, we can patriotically follow our government to war, and end up killing our neighbors instead of loving them. We can dutifully put up walls around our country to protect ourself in the name of national defense, but in the process can put our neighbors in a cage, or deport their children. We can follow our country's laws and take pride in being a law-abiding citizen, but in the process may participate in targeting neighbors to be unfairly incarcerated. We may vote with our constituents for what is best for our local interests, but in doing so may go against the best interests of our non-local neighbors.

Our loyalty to carnal and divine kingdoms will constantly be tested. When we follow God above everything, we prioritize being a loving neighbor and a faithful citizen of the kingdom of God.

MEDITATION

How often do you think of yourself as a citizen of the kingdom of God? How often do you feel your loyalty to Christ contradicts your country's policies and agendas? What are some current and historical examples of how your country failed to be Christlike?

Make it a common practice, even a weekly habit, to pledge your allegiance to Jesus.

PRAYER

God, I pledge my loyalty and allegiance to you. May I serve you and your kingdom above any country or government. Forgive me for the times I've been blinded by nationalism, and help me never to mistake my country, government, or partisan platform as being bigger or better than you.

I pledge allegiance to God Almighty,
Ruler of heaven, earth, and creation,
and to Christ's Kingdom, which I will serve:
all people, loved by God—
unfathomable, with mercy and justice for all.

⌐━━

The Idolatry of Nationalism

But seek first the kingdom of God and his righteousness.

—MATTHEW 6:33

AS CHRISTIANS, we are citizens of the kingdom of God. But a common roadblock to dedicating our lives to the kingdom of God by loving our neighbors to the best of our ability is the temptation to allow our allegiance to our country to supersede our allegiance to the kingdom of God—to succumb to nationalism.

Rather than viewing the world as a place filled with humans of unsurpassable worth who are made in the image of God, we can be guilty of categorizing people as citizens or non-citizens, immigrants and undocumented immigrants, refugees, outsiders, traitors, spies, and enemies. We adopt these labels from our politicians, media sources, and government. Instead of following the way of Christ as the ultimate blueprint for how to love God and love our neighbors, we can mistakenly follow patriotic propaganda.

It's easy for us to believe our own country is divinely favored, that it can do no wrong, that it *did* no wrong in the past, and that it's better than every other nation. This superiority complex venerates our nation's institutions, systems, and traditions, and it validates our political parties, military, government institutions, and historical documents. This can be a comforting lie to accept because it puts ourselves in the best possible light and exonerates us from any guilt or shame.

We can find great hope and comfort in nationalistic identities because they can provide a sense of corporate identity and purpose. It can be easy for us to turn nationalism into a false religion. We can deify national symbols as gods, and can become blinded by our devotion to our country. Nationalism can become another religion to us. When this happens we want everyone to conform to our personal assumptions, opinions, and worldview.

We may not even realize when we're participating in nationalism. Do we believe in the supremacy of our country and therefore the degradation of anyone who isn't a part of it? Do we hate and attack those who dare criticize it? Do we assume we're the best country in the world? Instead of celebrating the societal and economic successes of other countries, do we see them as a threat to our status? If your love of country is associated with a hate or fear of others, you're engaging in nationalism.

This concept of social justice is a common target for the ire of nationalists, because those who pursue social justice recognize the dignity of everyone, even those beyond their own national, cultural, religious, and socioeconomic identities. When we abide by the principles of social justice we celebrate the worth of everyone, even those who have different partisan, religious, philosophical, ethnic, racial, and cultural realities than our own.

Ever since Rome tried to quell the ministry of Jesus, nations—and their ardent worshipers—have tried to crush social justice, because its goals and ideals are contradictory to nationalism's aims of wealth, power, and domination. The work of social justice is the exact opposite of nationalism, the antithesis of exclusivity. It's inclusive because it's loving. By its very nature the pursuit of social justice cannot coexist with nationalism, which is why the two continually clash.

Under the right circumstances, usually through the brave leadership of extraordinary civil rights leaders and the determined grit of grassroots movements, a country may recognize the merits of social justice. Social justice advocates can be the impetus that extends human rights and creates a society that's more just, equitable, and loving. But just as often, nations and their governments suppress social justice for the sake of financial gain, political power, or pure selfishness. In these cases, they'll marshal all of their resources in a coordinated effort to destroy, delegitimize, defame, and stop social justice.

Nations and their nationalist devotees will attack social justice with a seldom-paralleled maliciousness. Social justice will be smeared as "unpatriotic" and "immoral." Religious nationalists will say it's too divisive, and their theologians argue that it's heretical. Nationalistic politicians will complain that it's too controversial, and businesses will lobby that it's too costly. Nationalist don't believe that time, energy, and money should be spent loving their neighbors, and they'll use any rationale to defend their attacks against social justice because they pursue their kings and kingdoms instead of Jesus (the King of kings) and his kingdom.

Religion and "Christianity" (a form of it that limits Christ) are common conduits of nationalism because they allow nationalists to pretend that their misguided passions are divinely ordained. In many cases, their hatred of others, along with their greed and bigotry and violence, is actually fueled by a spirituality baptized in racism, xenophobia, and ignorance. It's a religion that may be blinded by conspiracy theories, a revisionist national origin story, and an identity that assumes a quasi-divine right of power that is faultless. Nationalism uses the religious rhetoric of spirituality as a front for its oppression and injustice. When social justice work inevitably shatters this delusion, it is fiercely opposed. The police, national guard, and even army may be deployed to stop it. Pundits will smear it. Politicians denounce it. People will get tear-gassed, beaten, jailed, and shot. Nations don't give up their power easily.

Yet in spite of the riot gear, guns, tanks, and row upon row of armed military commandos, in spite of bloodied bodies, cold prison cells, and broken hearts, love and justice finds a way. It always wins in the end. The laws of God declare that it be so. And if not on earth, then at least in the afterlife. At the very least justice will reign, if not here and now, then for eternity. Jesus has already won, and with his victory justice cannot be evaded. Oppressors will receive judgment and injustice will face a reckoning. The great honor of social justice is to participate in such a divine process, to help bring about an eternal state of love and perfect justice.

Adoration for our country should never happen at the expense of us loving our neighbors. If our love of country inspires us to hate or fear others, we're no longer engaging in anything holy or good. We must practice disassociating from our national identities in order to fully embrace our identity in Christ.

Practice immersing yourself in a new identity, a divine one, an identity that is part of a different kingdom that prioritizes sacrifice and love over everything else. Because eventually, inevitably, our country will fail humanity. It will maim, oppress, and kill. We must daily, hourly, minute by minute make the conscious effort to pledge our allegiance to God's kingdom, which will never fail to love.

Social justice work denies nationalism for the sake of loving humanity, because sacrificially loving others is what Jesus did. Christ loved the world even though it gave him up to be brutally crucified by an empire—Rome—that believed in its own power, its own wealth, and its own gods. At first it appeared that Rome's power was greater, but only for a little while, for just three days, to be exact. . .

MEDITATION

But seek first the kingdom of God and his righteousness.
—MATTHEW 6:33

So are you? Are you seeking the kingdom of God first, or second, or at all?

But our citizenship is in heaven, and from it we await a Savior, the Lord Jesus Christ. **—PHILIPPIANS 3:20**

PRAYER

Dear God, I pledge my allegiance to you and your kingdom. May I not let my love of country, or my fear of others, ever prevent me from following one of your greatest commands: to love my neighbor.

DAY 13

⟵

Satan, Caesar, and Governments

"So give back to Caesar what is Caesar's, and to God what is God's."
—MATTHEW 22:21 NIV

This verse can be interpreted as a command to respect and obey governmental laws and authorities, but notice what Jesus is really saying: The things of God and the things of Caesar are *not* the same thing.

The Christian tradition sees God as the embodiment of good and Satan as the embodiment of evil. Everything bad, destructive, terrible, and deathly can be traced back to Satan, who is waging a cosmic battle against Jesus. In an epic showdown between these ageless enemies, described in Luke 4, Satan chose the Bible itself as the ultimate weapon to attack Jesus.

Just as Satan manipulated the context of Scripture to tempt Jesus, evil continues to manipulate Christians today by convincing us we're being biblical when in reality we aren't being like Jesus—or following his words—at all. Unfortunately, few things have been used to rationalize ungodly deeds, behavior, and horrors more than the Bible itself, and it's important for us to understand that it's way more important to be Christlike than it is to be "biblical."

Satan is a master theologian who has witnessed God, communicated and interacted with God, truly believes in God's existence, and knows and understands more about God than even the best biblical and theological scholars. But Satan doesn't *love* God. Satan abhors God, and because Satan hates God, Satan hates people.

When Satan tempted Jesus in the desert, he did so through a unique offer. Luke 4:5-8 describes Satan's plea:

> And the devil took him up and showed him all the kingdoms of the world in a moment of time, and said to him, "To you I will give all this authority and their glory, for it has been delivered to me, and I give it to whom I will. If you, then, will worship me, it will all be yours." And Jesus answered him, "It is written,
>
> "'You shall worship the Lord your God, and him only shall you serve.'"

In this passage Satan makes a surprising implication. Despite personally knowing (and experiencing) better than anyone the amount of power and strength Jesus yields, Satan confidently lays claim to controlling "all the kingdoms of the world and their glory." Jesus doesn't contradict this assertion, but instead declares that only God should be worshiped and served.

Although we know that God alone has ultimate authority in the universe, Scripture also suggests that Satan has some serious control over and within "kingdoms of the world." Jesus references Satan as "the ruler of this world" who "has no claim on me" (John 14:30). John states that the "whole world lies in the power of the evil one" and the apostle Paul adds that "the god of this world has blinded the minds of the unbelievers, to keep them from seeing the light of the gospel of the glory of Christ, who is the image of God" (2 Corinthians 4:4).

When Jesus says to give to Caesar what is Caesar's, he's declaring that the salvation, hope, and freedom that comes through the gospel of Christ won't come from Rome or any politician or political entity. Unlike the many Christian churches, leaders, and organizations who today spend their time, money, and energy trying to harness political power and seeking to influence the government to fit their religious agenda, Jesus didn't even attempt to appeal to Rome. He didn't lobby Rome's political leaders or create political action committees. He didn't cozy up to Caesar or run for office.

Instead, Jesus embodied social action and social justice through practical, sacrificial, and consistent love. This doesn't mean we shouldn't vote or use whatever influence we have to pursue the common good of others. Heroes like Martin Luther King Jr. and William Wilberforce used their faith to create positive changes and reform. But we should also note that the dehumanizing practices of racism and slavery they were fighting were implemented, facilitated, and promoted by "Christian" countries run by "Christian" governments. History continually serves as a sober warning of how easily the gospel can be co-opted to commit evil on behalf of others—especially ruling governments, armies, politicians, and religions.

By focusing on Jesus, we allow him to ultimately guide our thoughts and actions. If and when a country's government directly stands in opposition to the kingdom of God (as it often will), our allegiance to Jesus should trump our secondary allegiances to any other national government or institution, regardless of its legality, popularity, or prosperity. The kingdom of God is a loving entity we have the opportunity to serve above and beyond any earthly government, and Jesus is the king we have the honor to serve above and beyond any earthly ruler.

Peter and the other apostles replied: "We must obey God rather than human beings!" —**ACTS 5:29 NIV**

MEDITATION

Where does your allegiance lie? With your country or with the kingdom of God? How do these differ? Has your government ever stood in opposition to the words and actions of Jesus? Has it ever oppressed, villainized, and dehumanized others? Does your faith typically side with the oppressed or with those who are the ruling power? Identify one or more current laws or practices that are legal but contribute to social injustice. Think of one practical way you can contribute to ending this injustice.

PRAYER

God, again I pledge my allegiance to You. May your kingdom hold my loyal citizenship. Remind me that governments aren't always godly, and they routinely co-opt religion for their own agendas. May I never forget how civil rights movements, human rights movements, and peace movements have been adamantly opposed by government authorities and their laws, and opposed even by complicit churches and their theologies. Help me to value love and justice above all political and religious power.

DAY 14

Your World and the World

For God so loved the world, that he gave his only Son, that whoever believes in him should not perish but have eternal life. —**JOHN 3:16**

IT'S IMPORTANT to recognize that this iconic verse is written "For God so loved the world" and not "For God so loved America" or "For God so loved [insert your preferred country, religion, and political party]." God loves the world. God hates when we vilify outsiders and foreigners or name them as enemies. God loves them, and so should we.

Many large-scale injustices and forms of oppression are caused by foreign conflicts between nation-states. Wars, trade embargos, sanctions, military actions, exploitive business ventures, weapon distributions, and all sorts of dubious politicking have real consequences that impact the lives of millions of people. And if we aren't more intentional about being responsible for how our nation's foreign policies are created and facilitated, injustices will continue to grow to an unprecedented level.

In many ways, a collective ambivalence and apathy towards foreign policy and military conduct has caused and enabled major humanitarian problems around the world. We have a global refugee emergency, an immigration crisis, famines, food shortages and malnutrition, pandemics, medical deficiencies, violence and wars, human rights violations, political unrest, religious persecution, governmental suppression, poverty, and many other disasters happening right now, during our lifetimes. Unfortunately, many of these things have been brought about through our own national actions and policies. As an American, I can remember years ago when our country set off to "fix" Iraq and Afghanistan with bombs, fighting, and drone strikes. Much of my life has been lived with my country involved in those countries, dramatically altering the lives of people living there, with little to show for it. Yet we don't seem to take seriously the lessons of our national failures of military intervention, foreign policy, and diplomacy. There's a disconnect between the reality of the terror and suffering we inflict on other parts of the world and the reality of our comparatively comfortable and peaceful existence here in the United States.

Hopefully we can learn from our collective national mistakes, but also learn from other countries' successes. We can idolize our own country so much that we prevent ourselves from accepting the value and dignity of other states. When this happens, we may see ourselves as better than everyone else and remain ignorant of our own faults, unwilling to acknowledge or fix broken systems, policies, and ideals. This can cause a self-righteous mindset, preventing a country from progressing towards a more just and hopeful future because it is stuck in a self-inflicted echo chamber of ethnocentrism.

As Christians, our faith is a global collective of billions of people. To view Jesus only through one's own national identity, through the lens of a national agenda, is a grievous mistake that severely limits God's greatness. Jesus isn't American—or any other nationality—and

God's divine interests often contradict America's and any nation's national interests. Likewise, the work of social justice embraces a global conscience that honors the lives of those beyond our borders—those who will be impacted by either the good or bad results of our nation's actions and foreign policies. So let's strive for more humanitarian causes, where our nation's resources are spent uplifting the lives of others instead of ruining them. Let's try to stay informed and educated about the world and our global interactions. Let's collectively avoid nationalism and xenophobia and instead cultivate a corporate attitude of humility, goodwill, and peace.

MEDITATION

Do you ever think of your country as either better or worse than others? How does being a follower of Jesus affect the way you view people of the world?

"Cursed is anyone who denies justice to foreigners, orphans, or widows." And all the people will reply, "Amen."
—DEUTERONOMY 27:19 NLT

PRAYER

Dear God, I desire a mindset that sees everyone as created in your divine image, including everyone beyond my nation's borders, even those my government considers enemies. Remind me to follow your command to love my enemies, to love my neighbors, and to recognize that I serve your kingdom above my own.

DAY 15

Social Justice is Nonpartisan

Jesus answered, "My kingdom is not of this world."
—JOHN 18:36

For people will be lovers of self, lovers of money, proud, arrogant,
abusive, disobedient to their parents, ungrateful, unholy, heartless,
unappeasable, slanderous, without self-control, brutal, not loving
good, treacherous, reckless, swollen with conceit, lovers of pleasure
rather than lovers of God, having the appearance of godliness, but
denying its power. Avoid such people. **—2 TIMOTHY 3:2-5**

SOCIAL JUSTICE is neither liberal nor conservative, neither capitalist nor socialist. No political party, economic system, or form of
government has the market cornered on social justice. We may think
a democracy is better than a monarchy, or believe a heavily regu-
lated economy is better than a free market, but all of these systems
are equally susceptible to being co-opted by bad people or ruled by
good ones. Even the most well-intentioned governments and the best

political theories can be mismanaged, or broken, and can fail miserably. Every nation in the world has positives and negatives, but perfect utopias don't exist. Social justice supersedes all political, social, economic, and religious systems.

Nobody holds the exclusive rights to social justice, and social justice is thwarted when interpreted as a partisan agenda, or when it's only applied to—or exclusively associated with—specific people. Social justice can be done by the young or the old, the rich or the poor. A police officer, an activist, a CEO, a pastor, a teacher, a nurse, a lawyer, a politician, a parent, a social worker, a waitress, or a child; anyone can practice social justice. Social justice struggles when restricted by our own boundaries, and it must reflect the equity and fairness of God, not the skewed lines we use to segment groups and label people. Social justice work asks us to be impartial to our own preferred—yet imperfect—religious, political, and ideological beliefs. Social justice cannot be understood or pursued solely through the prism of our own biases, and its divine nature makes it a communal and holy ideal, something that cannot be owned or controlled by any one person, group, ideology, or partisan agenda.

It can be hard, but we are invited by God to humbly accept that our own religious communities, political parties, economic policies, government systems, and social structures are capable of injustice. Nobody is blameless—not even ourselves—so let's pray that our work is consistent in our pursuit so that when we encounter injustice we will be able to bring love, mercy, and justice to others, especially when it's needed within our very own country, political party, church, or family.

The pursuit of justice challenges us to have no double standards or ulterior motives. It shouldn't be used to harm the reputation of our enemies, or score political points for our favorite candidate, or spread a partisan agenda. Social justice work is a sacred responsibility, and we must be equally passionate about ending oppression whether we find the culprit of injustice to be a friend or foe. This is why pursuing social justice is easier for us when rooted in the love of Christ, because through the power of the Holy Spirit the miracle and mystery of love can be achieved.

MEDITATION

When are we most susceptible to bias, or to showing unfair preference for our particular beliefs or identity? How does politics help or hinder the work of social justice?

My brothers and sisters, believers in our glorious Lord Jesus Christ must not show favoritism. —**JAMES 2:1 NIV**

For God shows no partiality. —**ROMANS 2:11**

Finally, brothers and sisters, whatever is true, whatever is noble, whatever is right, whatever is pure, whatever is lovely, whatever is admirable—if anything is excellent or praiseworthy—think about such things. Whatever you have learned or received or heard from me, or seen in me—put it into practice. And the God of peace will be with you. —**PHILIPPIANS 4:8-9 NIV**

PRAYER

Dear God, may my pursuit for justice be honorable, pure, lovely, commendable, and just. May my thoughts, words, and actions be worthy of praise and truthful. Jesus, lead me through the powerful example of your life and words, and may the Holy Spirit guide me.

DAY 16

⟶

Jesus the Criminal

And when they came to the place that is called The Skull, there they crucified him, and the criminals, one on his right and one on his left.

—LUKE 23:33

CHRISTIANITY IS often represented by the symbol of a cross, which represents the manner in which Jesus was killed. The cross upon which Christ was crucified—at a place called "The Skull"—is an execution site. It was on crosses that countless criminals, enemies, and dissidents of the Roman Empire were gruesomely mutilated and killed. The modern equivalent of the cross would be a gurney with restrictive straps—the physical structure for those who are legally executed via lethal injection (which we call capital punishment) within the United States.

Imagine wearing a necklace with an electric chair instead of a crucifix, or going into a church where the altar is adorned with an elaborate execution chamber, showing a chair with straps that restrict a person to their deathbed, IV tubes for lethal injections dangling from its sides. Yet this is what the cross symbolizes in churches around the world. In displaying the cross, churches are proclaiming that their savior was legally executed by an empire as a criminal.

How easy it is to forget that Jesus Christ was an enemy of the state, arrested, incarcerated, tortured, proclaimed guilty according to the legal processes of that time, sentenced to a death via capital punishment, and crucified on a cross. The apex of the gospel—the crucifixion—is a story that symbolizes how Jesus and governments are almost completely contradictory to one another.

The good news is that Jesus was raised from the dead—saving humanity from sin. Though an empire striving for power through aggression inflicted evil upon him, his sacrificial love won victory.

Jesus pleads for peace while empires rush towards violence. Jesus demands love while empires spew hate. Jesus heals while empires torture. Jesus selflessly gives while empires selfishly take. Jesus invites inclusivity while empires operate on exclusivity. Jesus forgives while empires punish. The crucifixion reminds us that loyally following Christ is incompatible with loyally following a government—or the political parties that represent them. The more closely a person aligns with a ruling empire, the more difficult it becomes to follow Jesus.

When we prioritize patriotism and nationalism over faithfully emulating Christ's words and actions, we can exclude, fear, blame, villainize, ban, jail, and even kill our neighbors—whom we are called to love—under the guises of national security, foreign policy, economic strategy, and other manifestations that are constructed to serve partisan agendas rather than Christlike directives. When we worship the gods of "king and country" (who kill for us) over the divine God (who *was* killed for us) we are committing idolatry.

Although we worship the King of kings and Lord of lords, we must always remember that we also worship a convicted criminal. This will help us recognize the image of God in everyone we encounter, no matter their social, economic, or legal status.

MEDITATION

How does thinking of Jesus as a criminal change your perception of God? How does it affect the way you think of people today who are legally labeled as criminals?

PRAYER

Dear God, you are a convicted criminal, yet you are holy and good. May you help me not to judge others based on unjust laws and systems that are quick to punish the oppressed and maligned. You know injustice, and empathize with the incarcerated. Thank you for being a God of justice and mercy and hope and love.

DAY 17

Jesus the Heretic

While he was still speaking, Judas came, one of the twelve, and with him a great crowd with swords and clubs, from the chief priests and the elders of the people. Now the betrayer had given them a sign, saying, "The one I will kiss is the man; seize him." And he came up to Jesus at once and said, "Greetings, Rabbi!" And he kissed him. Jesus said to him, "Friend, do what you came to do." Then they came up and laid hands on Jesus and seized him. —**MATTHEW 26:47-50**

It was the religious leaders, with the help of a close personal friend of Jesus, who had Jesus arrested. This moment, when Jesus is betrayed by those who claim to worship God and handed over to be incarcerated and put to trial by the ruling empire, is an example of the ugly marriage between religion and political power. It is also an example of a common barrier to doing what's right within a system corrupted by power.

Those who pursue social justice with Christlike love will face similar obstacles, receiving opposition from religious leaders, angry crowds, politics, and ruling governments with their respective judicial, executive, and legislative branches. Even your family and friends may push back. You could get chastised, excommunicated, arrested, jailed, and even abandoned by those closest to you. Your fiercest battle may be against yourself, because your own mind and conscientiousness will struggle to undo bad habits, preconceived ideas, and old patterns that have been deeply entrenched.

Woe to those who call evil good and good evil, who put darkness for light and light for darkness, who put bitter for sweet and sweet for bitter! —ISAIAH 5:20

The Christlike practice of striving for social justice will often receive the most resistance from within Christianity itself. Those who benefit from injustice will use religion to morally and spiritually rationalize systems and practices that keep them in power. Since power and wealth are their idols, they will deify acts of injustice as being holy acts of God.

Thus the Christian religion can become a complicit oppressor rather than a Christlike witness. Throughout modern and ancient history, forms of Christianity have supported slavery, internment, sexism, torture, corruption, misogyny, bigotry, murder, genocide, racism, anti-Semitism, xenophobia, LGBTQIA+ discrimination, ageism, ableism, and countless other injustices. In many cases, it was the mainstream and majority-culture forms of Christianity that stood guilty of complicity. Entire societies and the systems that served as their frameworks—over countless generations—practiced a version of Christianity that inflicted injustice.

Rather than being religious heretics, social justice workers are disruptive changers: life changers, community changers, and world changers. They move us from slavery to freedom, from non-voters to voters, from separate drinking fountains to integrated ones, from lopsided salaries to equal ones, from being labeled illegal to being included as a citizen, from dehumanized to beloved human of unsurpassable worth. Social justice workers are visionaries who see beyond what always was, always is, and apparently always will be, to boldly imagine what should be, working until it actually *is*. They build a more Jesus-like reality.

Reworking and even eliminating the systems that oppress are sure to elicit strong reactions, especially from religious institutions that have historically benefitted from injustice. These carefully constructed systems are fiercely protected by social status, money, laws, and even armies. Social justice work destroys cruel status quos and topples the authorities that maintain them. The consequences of this are that people who benefit from the oppression of others, maybe even the vast majority of people in any given society, will turn on those pursuing social justice. The costs are high on both sides. The very humanity and dignity of people's lives are at stake. Oppressors will desperately cling to the wealth and power that injustice guarantees, and there will always be a price for participating in social justice. For many of us, the consequences of our social justice work will be that we're given labels such as *heretic* or *un-Christian*. But fear not, because just as Jesus faced fierce opposition from numerous religious leaders, so will we.

Social justice movements almost always begin as universally unpopular causes dismissed by almost everyone except the oppressed. Abolitionists. Suffragists. Civil rights leaders. Hated. Hated. Hated. Churches warned of their evil and heresy. Religions labeled social justice workers and activists as troublemakers and criminals and lawbreakers. But as the work progressed the resistance to social justice eventually faltered. Your social justice work may lead to social excommunication, legal action, incarceration, violence, and even death. Prepare yourself.

Mahatma Gandhi and Martin Luther King Jr. were assassinated. Dorothy Day was beaten by police, Nelson Mandela was imprisoned, Malala Yousafzai was shot in the head—but survived. Your reputation may be destroyed; you will lose friends, family, income, and even possibly your life. Jesus was arrested, tortured, and given the death penalty. Many of Christ's earliest followers faced similar fates. These are just a few of countless individuals who dedicated their lives to positive change.

Today is your day, but it is also your neighbor's day. Treat this shared existence within your place and time as a holy moment of communion, glorifying God through the pursuit of love and mercy, peace and kindness, hope and justice.

MEDITATION

Have you ever done something or believed something you considered Christlike that your church or friends thought was sinful? In what ways do you think social justice is mischaracterized by other Christians? In what ways do you think criticism of social justice is valid?

PRAYER

Dear God, help me to love my neighbor more than I love my Bible, defend the oppressed more than I defend my theological beliefs, and love humanity more than I love my religion.

Jesus the Immigrant, Jesus the Refugee

Behold, an angel of the Lord appeared to Joseph in a dream and
said, "Rise, take the child and his mother, and flee to Egypt, and
remain there until I tell you, for Herod is about to search for the
child, to destroy him." And he rose and took the child and his mother
by night and departed to Egypt. —**MATTHEW 2:13-14**

JESUS WAS AN IMMIGRANT and refugee, forced to flee with
his parents to Egypt from the murderous King Herod who sought to
kill them. Throughout history, countless people have had to leave their
homes for the sake of their well-being. Sometimes this is because of political or economic strife, sometimes it's due to rampant crime, and sometimes it's because of abuse and the threat of physical harm, or even war.

Jesus' family fleeing for their lives reminds us that to deny immigrants and refugees is to deny Christ. How can we serve a God who
mercifully grants us citizenship into the kingdom of God through no
merit of our own, yet deny immigrants and refugees a safe existence

within our own communities? How can we worship God for being our refuge, our comfort, our savior, yet simultaneously deny refuge, comfort, and literal life-saving help to immigrants and refugees? We can't. To be a follower of Jesus and a pursuer of justice means that we're Christlike in the way we advocate for those seeking a home.

The fate of immigrants and refugees often rests at the hands of governments. But as citizens of the kingdom of God, it's our sacred duty to extend love and mercy to them. To grant them asylum and citizenship, provide them with a safe haven, and welcome them into our communities because this is a loving gift—it is the way of Jesus. When we reflect on immigration and refugee policies, we need to support those that are loving towards immigrants and refugees, and oppose policies that oppose refugees and immigrants. Practice engaging in politics through having a heart like Jesus.

The plight of both immigrants and refugees centers on the idea of home—of both fleeing their old home and finding a new one. Having a space to call home offers stability and protection. It presents a place to be safe, to sleep, to eat, and to share a familial existence.

Loving immigrants and refugees as our neighbors accepts them fully within our communities and provides them with a home. It offers safety, citizenship, jobs, loving relationships, and a sustainable future. Instead of prioritizing profit or extortion, we have the chance to offer affordable housing, a safe shelter with food and water, and a sanctuary of peaceful longevity for the sake of loving our neighbor.

Just as Jesus offers us heaven and the kingdom of God as a home, a place of love and belonging, we can provide a home to those who need one.

MEDITATION

How do you think about Jesus differently when you think of him as an immigrant and refugee? How well do you think Jesus thinks your country treats refugees and immigrants? How well do you think you treat refugees and immigrants?

> When a foreigner resides among you in your land, do not mistreat them. The foreigner residing among you must be treated as your native-born. Love them as yourself, for you were foreigners in Egypt. I am the LORD your God.
> **—LEVITICUS 19:33-34 NIV**

PRAYER

Dear Jesus, you were an immigrant and refugee. May I love immigrants and refugees to the best of my ability and work on their behalf for their well-being, despite any resistance from my government or country's policies. God, may I always remember that immigrants and refugees are divinely created in your image, worthy of all my love. Thank you that despite any rejection from people, societies, or governments, you will always accept me and love me.

DAY 19

⟵

Jesus the Social Outcast

Now Peter was sitting out in the courtyard, and a servant girl came to him. "You also were with Jesus of Galilee," she said.

But he denied it before them all. "I don't know what you're talking about," he said.

Then he went out to the gateway, where another servant girl saw him and said to the people there, "This fellow was with Jesus of Nazareth."

He denied it again, with an oath: "I don't know the man!"

After a little while, those standing there went up to Peter and said, "Surely you are one of them; your accent gives you away."

Then he began to call down curses, and he swore to them, "I don't know the man!"

Immediately a rooster crowed. Then Peter remembered the word Jesus had spoken: "Before the rooster crows, you will disown me three times." And he went outside and wept bitterly.

—MATTHEW 26:69-75 NIV

IT'S HARD TO OVERSTATE how socially unpopular advocating for social justice can become. Jesus experienced this multiple times over. After befriending strangers and taking them on as his disciples, his reward for showing them how to serve and love others was betrayal and abandonment.

His closest friends and confidants, those he loved and cared for like family, eventually turned against him. Judas planned and carried out his betrayal, and Peter denied knowing him during his greatest time of need. Jesus' crimes: caring for the poor, feeding the hungry, healing the sick, and loving those whom society oppressed. Christ's pursuit of social justice upended his relationships, and it will happen to you, too.

You might lose Facebook friends, invitations to various social gatherings may cease, coworkers could shun you and relatives "ghost" you, all because of your "unreasonable" beliefs and actions. The loss of these relationships is often jarring and deeply painful. But if the cost of keeping these relationships means abandoning those who need our love the most—the sick, poor, oppressed, and maligned—then it's a price worth paying.

Evil thrives within communities too afraid of conflict, confrontation, and disruption. History's greatest horrors—concentration camps, genocides, slavery—relied on populations too timid to disrupt the status quo, who were too fearful to break from their pastors, community leaders, and political rulers. Conversely, all great civil rights revolutions began by individuals who did just that: who stood up for what was right even at great cost to themselves, losing family and friends in the process.

"Which of the two do you want me to release to you?" asked the governor.

"Barabbas," they answered.

"What shall I do, then, with Jesus who is called the Messiah?" Pilate asked.

They all answered, "Crucify him!"

"Why? What crime has he committed?" asked Pilate.

But they shouted all the louder, "Crucify him!"

—MATTHEW 27:21-23 NIV

By its very nature, social justice is unpopular. Massive government, social, religious, and economic systems are built upon injustice, and any effort to dismantle such structures will be met with widespread furor from those who benefit from the status quo.

Billions of dollars in profits, electoral political power, religious rule, and societal status are at stake. Those who benefit from injustice—usually the most influential segments of society—will do everything they can to dissuade, discourage, discredit, and defeat you.

This is why Jesus was branded a heretic and a criminal, and explains how a mob of people shouted "Crucify him!" and enthusiastically accelerated his public execution. These were the religious leaders and parishioners of his day, the politicians, the citizenry, demanding his death—for the sake of protecting their profits, power, and beliefs. When Pontius Pilate offered the crowds a choice between saving Jesus and Barabbas, the mob chose to free Barabbas—sending Christ to his gruesome death. Social justice work isn't going to win any popularity contests, so gird yourself for what is to come.

Will pursuing social justice require you to give up your life? Maybe. It's not uncommon for social justice activists around the world to get arrested, tortured, and even killed for their work. But even if you aren't killed, you'll most definitely face public backlash. You'll be teased, ridiculed, and shamed. Quite possibly, you'll be bullied, lose your job, and even be physically assaulted.

But what Jesus did—in his sacrificial life and death—was more important than popularity, wealth, and earthly power. It was a good and holy endeavor, just as it is for all who pursue social justice.

MEDITATION

Have you or someone you know ever faced opposition because of your social justice beliefs or work? Do you think social justice is accepted or opposed within Christian communities? Within society?

PRAYER

God, may I boldly pursue social justice regardless of the social, political, or financial costs. Regardless of the opposition I face, remind me that justice for others is far more valuable than my own comfort or pleasure. Thank you that your love cannot be defeated, and may any resistance to the love shown to my neighbors reinforce the truth that social justice is a holy work.

DAY 20

Jesus the Activist

The Spirit of the Lord is upon me, because he has anointed me to proclaim good news to the poor. He has sent me to proclaim liberty to the captives and recovering of sight to the blind, to set at liberty those who are oppressed, to proclaim the year of the Lord's favor.

—LUKE 4:18-19

THE SPIRIT OF GOD *liberates those who are oppressed.* God's very Spirit is not only against oppression but anoints us in the work of dismantling it.

As we strive to nudge the world towards a more peaceful and loving existence, recognize that historically, social justice has been a uniquely successful avenue of love, especially compared to other spiritual practices. Activists. Abolitionists. Boycotters. Strikers. Protestors. Sit-ins. Walk-outs. Marches. Speeches. Civil disobedience. Deep conversations and confrontations. Songs, and art, and poetry, and stories, and shared meals. It's these social actions, these deep human connections, that changed people's hearts and minds, which in turn helped change laws, and even changed society itself. It was social justice personified through the love of people.

Theology, Scripture, prayer, meditation, sermons, discipleship, and many other religious practices are deeply important to the Christian faith, but they're also regularly co-opted to oppress others, to discriminate, steal, and kill. But the work of social justice by its very nature serves to benefit others. Rather than being an empty religious belief, Christianity invites us into a holy form of activism. To act and be like Christ—to practice social justice—cannot be easily exploited.

Loving your neighbor has never led people astray. It's hard to think of a time in all of human history when sacrificial love has ever been construed as a bad thing by the people on the receiving end of that love. This is why social justice, of all the Christian disciplines and practices and traditions, has been dependably on the forefront of positive social change. Abolition. Desegregation. Women's rights. Voting rights. Workers' rights. LGBTQIA+ rights. Anti-racism. Environmentalism. All of these major human rights movements were led and instigated by social justice advocates, and few spiritual undertakings have put more emphasis on loving others than the pursuit of social justice.

God's precedent in both word and deed has already affirmed social justice as sacred, and we have the opportunity to reintroduce our churches to Jesus—the ultimate practitioner of social justice. When justice becomes the focal point of our faith, an admired and practiced discipline, we meaningfully represent Jesus within our communities.

As a pursuer of social justice, you may feel alone or even abandoned by institutional religion. But take heart, because God is with you. Jesus was an activist. He angered the religious leaders, created mobs, liberated, healed, accepted others, criticized Rome, chastised the powerful, and pursued justice, love, and mercy.

We love because Christ first loved us, and Jesus will be the last to love us, too, because his is an eternal love. His love will never fail or end. May that truth inspire us to love others in the same way Christ loves us.

MEDITATION

Do you think Christians who engage in social justice hurt or help the reputation of Christianity? How does your faith community participate in holy activism? What are some practical ways you can advocate for your neighbors?

PRAYER

Holy God, thank you for loving me, and help me to remember that in the same way you love me, you also love my neighbors, and even my enemies. May this verse be my prayer: "So we have come to know and to believe the love that God has for us. God is love, and whoever abides in love abides in God, and God abides in him" (1 John 4:16). May I love others so that I abide in you.

DAY 21

Jesus: The Prince of Peace

Then Jesus said to him, "Put your sword back into its place. For all who take the sword will perish by the sword. Do you think that I cannot appeal to my Father, and he will at once send me more than twelve legions of angels? But how then should the Scriptures be fulfilled, that it must be so?" —**MATTHEW 26:52-54**

SINCE SOCIAL JUSTICE reflects the heart of Christ, its strength manifests itself through peaceable love, not oppressive violence. Social justice seeks to protect life, not enact death. This is counterintuitive to nations that depend on martial strength and military supremacy as tools to forcibly enact their will upon others. War is the opposite of the fruit of the Spirit, bringing hate instead of love, sadness instead of joy, strife instead of peace, ferocity instead of patience, cruelty instead of kindness, treachery instead of goodness, violence instead of gentleness, and rashness instead of self-control. Families are torn apart, parents killed, children orphaned, cities flattened, trauma experienced. The wealthiest and most powerful are the most likely to escape harm—and may even accrue hefty profits from war—while the oppressed face the harshest of consequences.

War is theft. It steals innocent lives and destroys innocent minds. It diverts billions of dollars into the goal of raining death down upon others. Lives are stolen, and those who survive find their time, energy, emotions, and mental strength have been looted by nations, corporations, and powerful entities who care little for the costs yet greedily hoard the spoils. A person's entire being—all of their mind, body, emotions, and spiritual essence—was created to glorify God through acts of love, mercy, and justice, not to kill God's divine creations. War steals our souls.

God asks us to become peacemakers, to follow Jesus—the Prince of Peace—towards the path of love. War is the opposite of loving your enemy, but the work of social justice hopes to break our apathy towards perpetual war and violence. It longs for a future where our armies, weapons, and families, friends, and children are no longer invested in the destruction of others. Social justice can honor the bravery, sacrifice, and service of those within the military while still refusing to glorify violence or sanction the death of others. We love them so much that we don't want to lose them. Social justice sees through the lies of nationalistic propaganda and identifies our national enemies not as enemies at all, but as neighbors, as people made in God's image.

"Blessed are the peacemakers, for they will be called children of God," declares Jesus (Matthew 5:9 NIV). When you pursue social justice, your citizenship is to the kingdom of God, and its official currency is peace.

Our trust in peace directly reflects our trust in Jesus, who has the power of legions of angels at his disposal and yet insists on peace. Jesus is God incarnate, an omnipotent, omniscient, and omnipresent being. War and violence take the power of judgment away from God. When we turn to them, we assume that we know better than God and that we can bring about justice better than God—which is absurd.

Being peaceful is harder than being violent. Just look at the historical record of the world. Warriors, soldiers, and generals fill our history books, but only a handful of peaceful activists. It takes more fortitude, self-control, thoughtfulness, and heroism to be peaceful than it does to be violent. It's easy for us to hit back at someone who hurt us first, but it's an extraordinary act of courage and self-restraint when we can step back and attempt to defuse the situation, or to actually love our enemy.

Romans 12:17-21 instructs us to "repay no one evil for evil, but give thought to do what is honorable in the sight of all. If possible, so far as it depends on you, live peaceably with all. Beloved, never avenge yourselves, but leave it to the wrath of God, for it is written, 'Vengeance is mine, I will repay, says the Lord.' To the contrary, 'if your enemy is hungry, feed him; if he is thirsty, give him something to drink; for by so doing you will heap burning coals on his head.' Do not be overcome by evil, but overcome evil with good."

We tend to accept rhetoric about the virtues of being nonviolent, peaceful, and loving only until loving our enemy begins to feel difficult. Until someone is abused or assaulted. Or a terrorist bombs a public square. Or someone murders a loved one. An intruder breaks into our home and threatens the safety of our family. A country commits an act of war. We've been taught that the natural response to these circumstances is blood for blood.

But Jesus asks us to try a better way. When we walk in the way of peace, we see everyone as a divinely loved being. To see people as Jesus sees people is hard, and often seems illogical. But imagine the most love you've ever felt for someone in your entire life. Now imagine this love being amplified an infinite amount. This is the love that Jesus has for all people—for us and even for our enemies. Peacefulness may require creativity, or boldness, or even defy logic, but it's the Christlike way. If you don't believe me, believe Jesus, who chastised Peter for participating in an act of self-defense by defending Jesus when he violently fought those who were there to arrest Christ.

Peace isn't passive. Instead, it confronts the complexities of human nature and seeks alternative paths that avoid death and destruction. It's a heroic endeavor, requiring intelligence, bravery, and grit. Throughout Scripture we can see that Jesus was aggressively working towards peace. He healed people, he gave public speeches, he confronted religious leaders, he challenged Rome. He intervened on behalf of the oppressed, and eventually he even gave his own life for the sake of peace. Peaceful movements have actually been quite successful throughout history. Mahatma Gandhi revolutionized India, Nelson Mandela's eventual acceptance of pacifism transformed South Africa, and Martin Luther King Jr.'s nonviolent civil rights movement challenged America to face its sins and strive for a better path. But instead of aspiring to their incredible examples and normalizing peace, we have sanctioned violence as a necessity.

Jesus was—and is—the Prince of Peace. It's difficult to emulate the peacefulness of Christ, but it can be done. The Bible even celebrates courageous peace by highlighting Stephen's death, who was stoned to death by those who hated him, as we read in Acts 7:55-60:

> But he [Stephen], full of the Holy Spirit, gazed into heaven and saw the glory of God, and Jesus standing at the right hand of God. And he said, "Behold, I see the heavens opened, and the Son of Man standing at the right hand of God." But they cried out with a loud voice and stopped their ears and rushed together at him. Then they cast him out of the city and stoned him. And the witnesses laid down their garments at the feet of a young man named Saul. And as they were stoning Stephen, he called out,

"Lord Jesus, receive my spirit." And falling to his knees he cried out with a loud voice, "Lord, do not hold this sin against them." And when he had said this, he fell asleep.

Stephen could have fought back. Today such actions could be considered self-defense. But Stephen instead asked God to forgive his enemies, and echoed the exact words Christ spoke while on the cross: "Do not hold this sin against them." In documenting this event in Scripture, the author honors Stephen as the very first Christian martyr, and features Stephen's final words as a testament to his life and death: having the same character as Jesus, perfectly following what the Prince of Peace taught.

So today, practice being a peacemaker—a radical, illogical, countercultural peacemaker. In doing so, you practice being like Jesus.

MEDITATION

How do you feel about your country's recent or current military involvements? Were they justified? What were the good and bad results of them? Do you believe violence is ever okay?

Now may the Lord of peace himself give you peace at all times in every way. The Lord be with you all. —**2 THESSALONIANS 3:16**

If possible, so far as it depends on you, live peaceably with all.
—**ROMANS 12:18**

But I say to you, Love your enemies and pray for those who persecute you. —**MATTHEW 5:44**

PRAYER

Dear Prince of Peace, help me to be a peacemaker, bringing peace wherever I go and to whomever I meet. I want to value people more than my own gain of wealth or power. May I never misuse peace to avoid conflict or justice, or as a weapon to dismiss the oppression of others. Rather help me use peace as a process that brings truth, reconciliation, repair, and restorative love. Peace is hard, so I ask for a supernatural amount of perseverance, so that I can react in a Christlike way no matter the circumstance. God, thank you for being peaceful with me.

DAY 22

A Kingdom of God Mindset

From that time on Jesus began to explain to his disciples that he must go to Jerusalem and suffer many things at the hands of the elders, the chief priests and the teachers of the law, and that he must be killed and on the third day be raised to life.

Peter took him aside and began to rebuke him. "Never, Lord!" he said. "This shall never happen to you!"

Jesus turned and said to Peter, "Get behind me, Satan! You are a stumbling block to me; you do not have in mind the concerns of God, but merely human concerns."

—MATTHEW 16: 21-23 NIV

ONE OF THE HARDEST things about pursuing social justice is that it continually invites us to adopt the perspective of the kingdom of God rather than the kingdom of humankind. The divine concerns of God contradict the selfish motivations of humans, and this tension consistently manifests itself in our lives. But prioritizing the heart of God is so countercultural to our consumerist society that pursuing social justice becomes absurd to us when we've become used to living in a world where the well-being of others is rarely prioritized above our own.

In these verses, Peter is being completely normal and logical by most standards. He doesn't want Jesus to suffer or be killed. Surprisingly, instead of being grateful for this concern for his personal safety, Jesus rebukes Peter. He does this because Peter is missing the bigger picture.

Because what Jesus is doing is benefitting the entire world—literally saving it. He's defeating Satan and overcoming sin once and for all. Imagine if Jesus took Peter's words to heart and Peter convinced him to avoid the potential danger of pain, suffering, and death. The crucifixion never would have happened! There would be no resurrection, no defeat of death, no salvation, and ultimately no Christianity.

Fortunately, Jesus remained faithful to the kingdom of God. This is the challenge for all who do social justice: remaining faithful to the heart of God. The reasons to stop, quit, or compromise are numerous and often completely legitimate. The safe and sensible option that Peter presented Jesus as an alternative to dying on the cross was for all intents and purposes a valid choice. But Christ called it *Satanic*!

In the same way, the options to distract your time, energy, and action away from the pursuit of social justice will be many, and they will present themselves not as dangerous, contradictory, or hypocritical, but as inviting, well-meaning, and even attractive preferences to the work you have begun. Don't lose focus, and keep Jesus at the center of your life's calling. When you do this, the pursuit of social justice will always rise above the self-focused goals of career, wealth, popularity, and power.

> And a ruler asked him, "Good Teacher, what must I do to inherit eternal life?" And Jesus said to him, "Why do you call me good? No one is good except God alone. You know the commandments:

'Do not commit adultery, Do not murder, Do not steal, Do not bear false witness, Honor your father and mother.'" And he said, "All these I have kept from my youth." When Jesus heard this, he said to him, "One thing you still lack. Sell all that you have and distribute to the poor, and you will have treasure in heaven; and come, follow me." But when he heard these things, he became very sad, for he was extremely rich. Jesus, seeing that he had become sad, said, "How difficult it is for those who have wealth to enter the kingdom of God! For it is easier for a camel to go through the eye of a needle than for a rich person to enter the kingdom of God." Those who heard it said, "Then who can be saved?" But he said, "What is impossible with man is possible with God." And Peter said, "See, we have left our homes and followed you." And he said to them, "Truly, I say to you, there is no one who has left house or wife or brothers or parents or children, for the sake of the kingdom of God, who will not receive many times more in this time, and in the age to come eternal life.

—LUKE 18:18-30

It's easy to get distracted by our own goals rather than wholly commit to pursuing the kingdom of God. The rich young ruler was a good person. He knew the commandments and followed them accordingly. He was probably an upstanding citizen in his society. If he were alive today, he'd probably be an elder at his local church, manager of a successful business, and coach of his kid's soccer team.

But Jesus knew what you may have already come to realize about all systems of injustice: they exist, expand, and even thrive among good people. Unjust societies are built on good and normal people doing "good" and "normal" things: Law-abiding citizens who passively watch as a person of color gets stopped and frisked. Officers who dutifully arrest those in possession of various ounces of illicit drugs, and judges who faithfully impose the mandated high sentences, but both of which are legislated policies meant to be more punitive towards people of color. Corporate executives who manage large businesses, yet who oversee human resource departments that hire a disproportionate amount of White men—and pay women employees substantially less. Educators who obediently grade students based on required standards, and colleges who evaluate admission applications upon tests and academic marks, but are done within academic systems that favor students of the dominant culture, or give an unfair advantage to students who can afford various benefits such as laptops, learning programs, tutoring, and extra-curricular development opportunities. Soldiers who follow orders to drop bombs at specific locations, yet the orders serve the profiteering agendas of large multinational corporations.

But God is looking for moments of greatness from us. Pursuing social justice requires us to go from good to great. We must no longer be complacent to the passivity of injustice being acceptable, no longer accept inequality or passively avoid the realities of discrimination and oppression. Instead, God desires people who will refuse to compromise to the injustices of our world.

When we look at the horrific atrocities of world history, there are obvious villains: dictators, fascists, and genocidal maniacs. But millions of good and decent people were also complicit in their evil machinations. Whether through coercion, threat of violence, ignorance, enlistment, legislative orders, populism, or simple complacency, history's darkest movements required masses of ordinary people to help manifest the oppression. All that injustice required was for huge segments of the population to do nothing, to believe in whatever excuses they told themselves in order to sit back and refuse to act.

Right now, you're living within the same time and spaces as somebody's darkest moment of oppression. Social justice requires us to find that person and save them from it.

MEDITATION

Is there an area of your life where you're prioritizing your own goals rather than the goals of the kingdom of God? How can you maintain a mindset of actively being a part of God's kingdom? What are some common distractions or roadblocks that prevent you from having a kingdom of God mentality?

But be doers of the word, and not hearers only. —**JAMES 1:22**

PRAYER

Dear God, I pray for a kingdom mindset. Please renew my mind so that I follow Jesus above all else. Make my desire to be like Christ enable me to help people overcome oppression just like you have helped me. I don't want to be passive or apathetic: give me the courage to be a passionate activist. Guide my actions and show me favor as I battle against oppression. Just as Jesus made a positive difference, may I also work to change the society I live in so that it will be more loving.

Made in God's Image

So God created human beings in his own image. In the image of
God he created them. **—GENESIS 1:27 NLT**

EVERY SINGLE PERSON is made in the divine image of God
(*imago Dei*) and loved by God. This belief in the value and worth of all
humans is the cornerstone of social justice. All forms of oppression and
injustice are the result of people not being treated as they deserve to
be: as divine image-bearers of God. Social justice is necessary because
people are lovingly made in God's image. Not even angels, entities that
seem to have more supernatural power and ability than humans, are
given this distinguished honor. So why do we treat our fellow humans
so badly? Why are we so apathetic to their pain and suffering?

Injustice relies on dehumanization to make oppression more tol-
erable and acceptable. If we don't really believe that people are worth
that much, then it becomes easier to live in a world where they're mistreated. Social justice work encourages us to stand against all forms
of dehumanization, because people aren't animals, monsters, or "an

infestation." They're not a drain on the economy or a threat to our existence. They aren't property or possessions. They're not illegal. They're not disgusting or less-than. They're not third-world or low caste or any other oppressive hierarchical label.

There's a continuum to how we value people. On the one side, we can view them as not being people at all—less than human, inhuman—and this view allows us to rationalize behavior we wouldn't otherwise deem moral: to distrust, hate, scapegoat, enslave, and kill. We dehumanize based on cultural, religious, political, and even the most superficial differences. On the other side of the spectrum is the Jesus way, Christ's reality of seeing everyone as divinely created in the image of God, a holy being loved by God. Loved so fiercely by Jesus that it points to Christ's own crucifixion: a sacrificial death undertaken out of love.

Us. vs. Them. Allies vs. Enemies. These two narratives constantly battle for our hearts, souls, and minds, warring to determine how we'll treat—and think about—others (and how others treat us). Each day we must decide whether to treat people with love or hate, mercy or apathy, justice or injustice. When we use generalizing pronouns like "them" or "those people," we must always remember who "they" are: divinely loved individuals who are made in God's image. We must learn to see people as human beings, not as academic studies, or partisan pawns, or religious converts, or whatever labels, associations, and stereotypes we're prone to attach to them. No, social justice work welcomes us to honor every single person as a divine image bearer of God, loved by God, and definitely deserving of our own love.

MEDITATION

Do you view every person as made in God's divine image? Do you think God loves everyone? How does this change the way you think about them? Have you ever witnessed dehumanization? What forms have you seen this take?

PRAYER

God, may I love as you love. And help me to see everyone as you see them: lovingly made in your divine image. I want to treat others with the honor, respect, and dignity that they deserve. For even the hardest people to love, show me their divine worth. Erase my assumptions, prejudices, and stereotypes that prevent me from loving others. And even as I learn to accept others as being made in your image, may I accept that truth for myself, and realize that you love me, too, with the same unending love that you give others.

Sexual and Gender Prejudice

For you formed my inward parts;
    you knitted me together in my mother's womb.
I praise you, for I am fearfully and wonderfully made.
Wonderful are your works;
    my soul knows it very well.
My frame was not hidden from you,
when I was being made in secret,
    intricately woven in the depths of the earth.
Your eyes saw my unformed substance;
in your book were written, every one of them,
    the days that were formed for me,
    when as yet there was none of them.

—PSALM 139:13-16

LOVE, MERCY, AND JUSTICE should never be withheld or withdrawn because of gender identity, gender expression, or sexual orientation. Injustice is when anyone, for any reason, is treated as if they are not worthy of love.

God loves LGBTQIA+ individuals. Each is a divine creation, made in God's image. God loves him, her, you, us, they, and them. No matter a person's sex, gender, expression, or orientation, Jesus loves everyone, and those who pursue social justice are invited to love everyone, too. Social justice is inclusive because Jesus is inclusive. This must especially be true when anyone faces discrimination or bigotry because of sexual prejudice.

Open your heart to God's love. Realize this love. Meditate on this love. Accept this love. Rejoice in this love. This love is a divine truth. It cannot be undone or withdrawn. It is timeless and eternal. It isn't reluctant or obligatory. It's not automatic or disinterested. It's deserved. It's passionate. It's infinite. It belongs to him, her, you, us, they, and them. It's yours.

LGBTQIA+ Christians are full members of the church and should be honored as such. But many systems of religion oppress LGBTQIA+ individuals and use faith to rationalize injustices. This mistreatment is often spiritualized as upholding divine laws or saving people from sinful lifestyles, but it is actually an oppressive form of power, control, and subjugation. The hypocrisy and complicity of Christianity's oppression of LGBTQIA+ individuals must also be fully acknowledged and confronted.

Mainstream Christianity's failure to love LGBTQIA+ individuals points up the importance of social justice, which loves others even when the majority of Christians won't. Social justice work is the Christlike conscience to a religion constantly trying to escape the humble savior it routinely tries to abandon. For Christianity, social justice is often the more difficult road, a route disapproved by some theologians, pastors, and denominations, but one that follows Jesus nonetheless.

MEDITATION

> For I am sure that neither death nor life, nor angels nor rulers,
> nor things present nor things to come, nor powers, nor height nor
> depth, nor anything else in all creation, will be able to separate us
> from the love of God in Christ Jesus our Lord.
>
> **—ROMANS 8:38-39**

How does your local Christian community love—or not love—LGBTQIA+ individuals? How can Christians atone for our past injustices against them?

PRAYER

God, thank you for creating me uniquely, knowing who I truly am even if others don't. I praise you for creating others uniquely, and I pray that everyone will lovingly accept themselves for who they are. I celebrate and accept your passionate love for myself and others. Help me stand against all forms of bigotry and sexual prejudice. May I fight against oppression and injustice that attacks people based on their sexual orientation, gender identity, and gender expression. Just as you are my advocate and ally, may I be an advocate and ally to LGBTQIA+ individuals.

DAY 25

Becoming Anti-Racist

When the day of Pentecost arrived, they were all together in one place. And suddenly there came from heaven a sound like a mighty rushing wind, and it filled the entire house where they were sitting. . . .

And at this sound the multitude came together, and they were bewildered, because each one was hearing them speak in his own language. And they were amazed and astonished, saying, "Are not all these who are speaking Galileans? And how is it that we hear, each of us in his own native language? Parthians and Medes and Elamites and residents of Mesopotamia, Judea and Cappadocia, Pontus and Asia, Phrygia and Pamphylia, Egypt and the parts of Libya belonging to Cyrene, and visitors from Rome, both Jews and proselytes, Cretans and Arabians—we hear them telling in our own tongues the mighty works of God." And all were amazed and perplexed, saying to one another, "What does this mean?" —**ACTS 2:1-2, 6-12**

FOLLOWING JESUS requires opposition to all forms of racism. To be Christlike is to be *anti*-racist. Fighting racism is an act of holiness, a privilege of the highest order. The Holy Spirit desires all people to be treasured as God's divine image-bearers, and racism directly contradicts God's love for humanity. We see this at Pentecost, the celebration of the day the Holy Spirit was given as a gift to the church, when the Holy Spirit bestowed people from different nations—who were very different in beliefs, cultures, ethnicities, and skin color—the divine ability to communicate with and understand each other.

"And all were amazed and perplexed, saying to one another, 'What does this mean?'"(Acts 2:12). What *does* this mean? That the Holy Spirit's very first manifestation to the church was a miraculous act of cross-cultural communication that serves as a timeless spiritual precedent for radical inclusivity. It's as if the Spirit of God was omnisciently predicting a future filled with racism and oppression, in which humans would create the idea of race as a hierarchical social construct, using these human-made categories as weapons to degrade people as inferior, to make assumptions about others, to hate people and violate them, to enslave and degrade them, even to murder them.

Racism is a state of being. It's our holistic self—our words, thoughts, and actions—either promoting equity or inequity, either helping or hurting others. Unfortunately, racism has been institutionalized by schools, businesses, judicial and incarceration systems, governments, and entire societies. Our governmental, law enforcement, military, entertainment, economic, religious, educational, and societal systems and policies are racist. They were created to be this way.

Worst of all, our churches and our very religion have embraced and spread racism. We have theologically defended it, spiritualized it, and religiously disguised it. Christians throughout history have sanctioned genocide, colonialism, slavery, segregation, internment, anti-immigration, and countless forms of hate and violence because we've been poisoned by racism, even baptizing these horrors as forms of Christianity. Many segments of our religion profited from slavery and have used racism as a tool for acquiring political power. Instead of loving our neighbors, we have hated them. This not only breaks our fellowship with our fellow humankind, but with God. Racism blasphemes against the Holy Spirit and takes God's name in vain.

The severity of racism may tempt us to refute its existence or avoid its presence within our own faith traditions. But doing so rejects the reality of our neighbors who experience racism. To negate the prevalence of racism is to diminish the worth of millions of our neighbors who suffer from its oppression. Anti-racism work embodies the divine call to love others. "For the whole law is fulfilled in one word: "You shall love your neighbor as yourself" (Galatians 5:14). To love our neighbors is to fully accept them, and to fully accept the reality of the oppression they face.

Many deny the existence of racism. They ignore and revise historical truths about the evils of slavery, lynchings, and racist policies, and then deny the overwhelming facts, witnesses, and research proving the existence of systemic racism within present-day society. Embracing false narratives and alternate realities are futile attempts to negate one's culpability for racism. Raising awareness and educating others about racism, and recognizing the historical and modern consequences of colonization, is participating in truth. Despite accusations of being a form of Marxism, race-baiting, or politicking, the discipline of becoming anti-racist is a holy endeavor of becoming more like Jesus.

The work of anti-racism begins with ourselves. We must admit our own racism, identify our own biases, and constantly strive to love our neighbor better. We must commit to combating it within our very hearts, souls, and minds.

We see the fruit of this in the post-Pentecost church, described in Acts 2:43-47:

And awe came upon every soul, and many wonders and signs were being done through the apostles. And all who believed were together and had all things in common. And they were selling their possessions and belongings and distributing the proceeds to all, as any had need. And day by day, attending the temple together and breaking bread in their homes, they received their food with glad and generous hearts, praising God and having favor with all the people.

The way of Jesus is to be in awe of others, to love them, not to hate them. Through the power of the Holy Spirit, may we be holy and righteously anti-racist.

MEDITATION

How might your words, thoughts, or actions be complicit in racism? How can you actively be anti-racist? How do you envision the physical appearance of Jesus? Do you see him as a person of color? Does the physical appearance of Jesus matter? Why or why not?

Do not judge by appearances. —**JOHN 7:24**

PRAYER

Holy Spirit guide me, and please remind me daily that Jesus wasn't a White Anglo-Saxon, but an Aramaic-speaking Middle Eastern ethnic minority living under Roman rule. May I see the image of God in everyone: my friends, strangers, enemies, foreigners, no matter who they are, what they look like, or where they come from. Whatever their nationality, skin -color, origin, or background, may I love them. Give me the strength to destroy racist systems and end racist policies, and to love my neighbor as I would myself.

DAY 26:

The Beautiful Diversity and Inclusivity of God

After this I looked, and behold, a great multitude that no one
could number, from every nation, from all tribes and peoples and
languages, standing before the throne and before the Lamb,
clothed in white robes, with palm branches in their hands.

—REVELATION 7:9

WHO IS PART of your Christian community? What ages, cultures, and demographic characteristics are represented? The verse from Revelation shows us the wonderful inclusivity and diversity of what God's community will ultimately be like. It should serve as a perfect example of what our religious ethic should strive for.

Although Christianity is as diverse and nuanced as the billions of people in the world that represent it, we tend to congregate with those who share similar beliefs and practices. It's tempting to surround ourselves with people who look like us, live like us, and share the same ethnic, cultural, political, economic, and social characteristics as us. An ethnocentric faith prefers comfort within familiarity, and is satisfied by similarities, interpreting a homogeneous religious community as a validation of truth and superiority rather than the severely limited reality that it is. When we isolate ourselves within insular communities—intentionally or not—we miss out on one of the most beautiful and wondrous experiences God has for us: the full awesomeness of joining together with all the diverse people created in God's image.

Social and spiritual ethnocentrism is often driven by prejudice and fear, and it prevents us not only from loving humanity, but also from loving God who diversely created. It leads to narcissism, pride, and ignorance. We can mistake ethnocentrism for church tradition, protecting us from any attack on our theological doctrines or protecting specific faith practices from outsiders. This also allows us to dismiss any insider who dares to challenge the status quo. By refusing to honor, value, and love those who are different from us, we're hindering our capacity for wisdom, knowledge, spiritual growth, and relational maturity. Sameness isn't an effective strategy for knowing God, and it invalidates our unique one-of-a-kind personhood.

When we look at the life of Jesus, we often miss an obvious truth about his ministry—how he facilitated interactions between a wide variety of people across various sections of society, inspiring them to communicate with each other, know each other, learn to understand each other, and ultimately love each other. He introduced Jewish people to Samaritans, the poor to the rich, the Romans to the non-Romans, the disciples to the Pharisees, the sick to the healthy, the hungry to the well-fed, the Jews to the Gentiles, the adults to the children, the socially powerful to the socially maligned, the oppressed to the oppressors, the free to the enslaved, the jailed to the jailers, and the friends to their enemies. And Jesus socialized with tax collectors, prostitutes, soldiers, criminals, and everyone in between. Again and again, Jesus is crossing social barriers, gender stereotypes, institutional norms, and religious expectations in order to connect people, people who never would have otherwise interacted with each other.

In Galatians 3:26-28 we read, "for in Christ Jesus you are all sons of God, through faith. For as many of you as were baptized into Christ have put on Christ. There is neither Jew nor Greek, there is neither slave nor free, there is no male and female, for you are all one in Christ Jesus."

These verses recognize the real differences between people and at the same time affirm God's inclusive love for everyone. Some are Jews while others are Greek, some are free while others are enslaved, and some are male while others are female. In that specific time and place, these distinctive identifiers had huge connotations that impacted everyday existence, affecting the way people lived and interacted with each other. Despite these huge cultural differences that everyone would have known and recognized, God is saying that in Christ we are all beloved and accepted, and thus we should all love and accept each other, no matter how great our differences. Likewise, God wants us to embrace one another while recognizing these differences and intentionally reaching across them, too. God is saying that our communities should reflect the very complex and diverse world that surrounds us.

Too often we settle for tokenism or superficial inclusion in our churches. Maybe our community is multicultural, or has a diverse population of people, but this doesn't mean anything if there's not real equity, justice, and love. We practice tokenism and superficial inclusion when we prevent individuals of different cultures from leadership positions, or pay them less, or ignore their justice causes, or simply treat them as less-than, and ultimately expect them to conform to the dominant culture rather than embrace and lead from their own.

Wait. Does this mean that we're expected to give up our own preferences, positions of power, pay, time, space, and resources for the sake of others, just because they're of a different gender, culture, or socio-economic makeup? Yes.

If you're in a position of leadership within Christianity, think of ways to give up your space and position in order to promote the beautiful diversity created by God—for the sake of glorifying God. This could mean giving your speaking engagements to others, resigning your leadership position and giving it to someone else, taking a pay cut so someone else can have an equal salary, and even sacrificing your job, friends, and reputation in order to pursue social justice. These are all practical ways to be more equitable, justice-minded, and loving.

MEDITATION

Does your faith community celebrate diversity or prefer ethnocentricity? Is the worship, teaching, and overall structure of your church designed for a particular group at the expense of ignoring or excluding others? How can you and your faith community better accept the differences of others?

PRAYER

God, I recognize that Christianity is made up of billions of different people. Thank you for valuing me for who I truly am, and not forcing me to be someone I'm not. You love me, and you love my neighbors. May I love all of my neighbors, both those who are like me and those who are different from me. You created everything and everyone, and are all-knowing, all-present, and all-powerful, yet you included me. You see me as special and love me as such. May I include others and love them just as you have done with me.

Children and the Elderly

But Jesus said, "Let the little children come to me and do not hinder them, for to such belongs the kingdom of heaven."
—MATTHEW 19:14

Father of the fatherless and protector of widows is God in his holy habitation. **—PSALM 68:5**

CHILDREN HELPLESSLY experience the consequences of humanity's greed, hate, and violence. Hundreds of millions of children around the world live in poverty, millions of children are refugees, and millions more are trafficked for sex and labor. Children everywhere face physical and sexual abuse, malnourishment and hunger, a lack of education, homelessness, and all sorts of emotional and mental trauma.

All children—and adults—should have access to proper healthcare, education, food, and shelter. But unlike adults, children aren't capable of being responsible for their own economic, social, and physical circumstances. The common arguments used against those in need of social justice cannot be used against children; we can't blame the bad things that happen to them on their poor life decisions, morality, or political preferences.

Children are at the mercy of our stewardship. We are their charges and custodians, guardians of their physical, emotional, intellectual, and spiritual well-being, and we are asked by God to prioritize their welfare. The state of any society can be judged by how it values and protects the health and progress of its children.

To pursue social justice for children is to reflect the truth that God is on their side. Jesus, while explaining the value of children to his disciples, firmly declared, "See that you do not despise one of these little ones. For I tell you that in heaven their angels always see the face of my Father who is in heaven" (Matthew 18:10). His teachings to the disciples are just as applicable to us: children are extremely important, to be cherished, valued, and admired. Children are spiritually vibrant, having the hearts and minds that God desires us to have. Social justice work protects and cares for them, but children also deserve our deepest respect, and we can humbly learn from them. They embody earnestness, truth, and the ability to be express themselves fully. They are passionate and bold, brave and honest, and they often represent kindness, mercy, and love towards others better than anyone.

Do not cast me off in the time of old age; forsake me not when my strength is spent.—**PSALM 71:9**

The work of social justice is built upon community, blessing us with deep and meaningful relationships. If one group is left out or forgotten, try welcoming them in and ensure their belonging. One group that often ends up in this position is those whose lives are nearing their end.

During times of crisis or scarcity, we often sacrifice the health, safety, and wellness of older people: "They've already lived a long life, so we should prioritize the young" has been a rationale used during worldwide pandemics. Though older people were significantly more at risk and died at much higher rates during the COVID-19 pandemic, many who were young and relatively healthy downplayed the tragedy and were unwilling to sacrifice their time, energy, and commitment for the health and safety of the elderly.

The social injustice of income inequality rears its ugly head as we age. As our bodies wear down, healthcare, personal care, housing, and other costs can become substantial. Those without good insurance, or proper medical accommodations, or retirement funds, are left wanting. The radical disparity of how the elderly live out their final days often reflects the injustices of our society.

How we spend our time, and whom we spend it with, reflects our values. The elderly are often an afterthought, cut out from our communal life through technological advances, loss of mobility, and what many perceive as a lack of influence or value. Many elderly suffer from a sense of isolation and abandonment. Ageism is real. Whether it's the way we do church, communicate, or socialize, we can discriminate against those who are older. When we forsake the elderly, we are missing out on the joy, peace, and love they bring into the world. Social justice work practices the discipline of intentionally shaping our lives and our faith communities to value the wisdom, experience, and life the elderly offer us.

MEDITATION

Wisdom is with the aged, and understanding in length of days.

—JOB 12:12

"You shall stand up before the gray head and honor the face of an old man, and you shall fear your God: I am the Lord."

—LEVITICUS 19:32

Behold, children are a heritage from the LORD. —**PSALM 127:3**

Listen to your father who gave you life, and do not despise your mother when she is old. —**PROVERBS 23:22**

Reflect on both the elderly and children within your family, faith community, and neighborhood. How might they feel cut out or left behind? How can you strengthen your relationships with them?

PRAYER

Dear God, help me never to dismiss people based on their age or ability. Help me to care for children and the elderly, and to take up their causes of injustice. Thank you for the wisdom of children and the aged, and give me enough humility to recognize their worth and learn from them both. I pray that I'll commit my time, energy, and space for them. They are a blessing to me, and may I treasure their presence in my life and celebrate my relationships with them.

DAY 28

Ableism

You shall not curse the deaf or put a stumbling block before the
blind, but you shall fear your God: I am the LORD.

—LEVITICUS 19:14

ABLEISM IS SOMETHING many Christian communities have yet
to address. Justice work around racism and environmentalism are more
common within churches, but for the most part Christianity caters to,
and centers itself upon, those who are able-bodied. Ableism is one of
the most prevalent forms of discrimination, yet it remains an injustice
lacking the exposure and weight it deserves.

Spiritual rhetoric, and even the way we exegete biblical texts, are
often extremely ableist, filled with insulting, derogatory, and dehumanizing imagery that assumes the superiority of people with typical abilities. We can throw around terms like *deaf* and *blind* and associate them
with iniquity and sin, stigmatizing common disabilities by unwittingly
attaching them to the idea of spiritual depravity. Churches can insinu-
ate physical ability—and healing—equate with righteousness and holy

merit, as if disability is a sign of something lacking. Many Christian traditions have also idolized the concepts of healing and wholeness to the point of ostracizing the disabled by presenting ableist physicality and health as the ideal model of God's intent for people. Christianity has yet to normalize disabled theologians and church leaders, and although we may theologically admit disabled people as being fully human, in reality we've created a religion of inaccessibility and malignment.

Just as it was in Jesus' time, ableism is so prevalent within our society that we don't even recognize it, like when a movie villain has a face that's deformed, a common trope that insinuates that an abnormality is associated with being bad and evil.

Jesus speaks boldly against these myths and social stigmas. He dispels the idea that illnesses, or physical and mental disabilities, are a sign of sin. In John 9:2-3, Jesus is asked, "Rabbi, who sinned, this man or his parents, that he was born blind?" Jesus answered, "It was not that this man sinned, or his parents . . ." Jesus is trying to teach an ableist society to value people beyond their physical disabilities.

Unfortunately, it didn't work. Despite relentlessly preaching a message that everyone is fully human and fully loved by God, people continued to categorize and exclude others based on ability, health, social status, and countless other factors—a trend that continues to this day.

Have you ever uttered one of these words: *moron, idiot, imbecile, crazy, lame, crippled, retard, libtard, insane, triggered?* This kind of language diminishes human experiences or degrades human worth, and we must immediately stop using it. Words matter. So do our actions. Educate yourself on ableism and the kinds of barriers and inequality people with disabilities face. Read, learn, listen, dialogue, and engage in meaningful relationships with them. Then do something about it. Fight for accessibility and equity.

Jesus is a God of accessibility. He doesn't obstruct, omit, or exclude. God knows people for who they actually are: not less-than or needing to be fixed, but amazing, phenomenal, extraordinary individuals. Rather than experiencing prejudice and discrimination, people with disabilities deserve to be honored, loved, and treasured for their unique gifts, able to hold positions as leaders, role models, mentors, teachers, and contributors.

Likewise, our churches and facilities have the opportunity to be as accommodating and accessible as possible, places of true belonging. The ideal of social justice inspires faith communities to see the value and power of people with disabilities—not to seek exemption from legal mandates, or to do just the bare minimum to meet legal compliance requirements, or to cater programming only to those with typical abilities.

For faith communities, accessibility is an area where they can lead others, centering disability access for every building design, program implementation, ministry vision, social function, and organizational structure. Our love for others draws us to be at the forefront fighting ableism within our work life, social life, spiritual life, and everyday life. Let's find ways to be inclusive to those who are different from us.

MEDITATION

Do you have friends or family who suffer from the obstructions and discrimination of ableism? In what ways might your church or faith community be inaccessible to people with disabilities? How can you make your community more accessible and welcoming?

PRAYER

God, help me to realize my biases. I pray that I will fight for disability rights and against ableist discrimination. Forgive me for my ableist tendencies, and help me overcome my ignorance. May I never idolize typical abilities, and may I never be prejudiced against or in any way exclude those who have a disability.

Humbly Educate Yourself

Let the wise hear and increase in learning, and the one who understands obtain guidance. —**PROVERBS 1:5**

But the Helper, the Holy Spirit, whom the Father will send in my name, he will teach you all things. —**JOHN 14:26**

Before you act, it's wise to first learn, which will then inspire you to action. God is a teacher, and Christianity is a lifelong journey of accruing wisdom and knowledge, a pilgrim's progress of emotional, spiritual, and intellectual growth. The pursuit of social justice is a permanent dedication to learning, teaching, and doing. We learn what we don't yet know in order to overcome our ignorance, then teach what we've learned to others and practice the discipline of bringing justice to others. One of the great gifts of social justice is that it brings wisdom, guidance, and knowledge to humanity. It's a truly holy moment when foolishness is replaced with wisdom, when we're guided onto a path of justice and love, and when our ignorance is defeated through knowledge. Accomplishing these things is grueling work, but it will give us a humble and patient heart.

Social justice is connected to many causes, ideals, platforms, and people. It's impossible to know everything about all of them. Experts in one area may be amateurs in another. For example, someone who has dedicated their entire life to the issue of affordable housing in Detroit may not know a single thing about deforestation in the Amazon rainforest. There are countless injustices that we'll know nothing about, and many times we'll be too woefully uninformed to help. And that's okay, because our souls are incapable of handling all of the world's injustices at once. We're not created to take on such an unfathomable burden. Instead, God has given each of us unique passions, bestowed us with particular skills and gifts and talents, and placed us within distinct circumstances in order that we can participate in social justice in our own special way. This doesn't give us an excuse to sit on the sidelines during a crisis or remain willfully ignorant, it's just acknowledging the fact that the world is a vast place filled with innumerable injustices that we'll never fully know or understand.

Justice work allows us to educate ourselves with what's happening around us, seeking to better understand the oppression affecting our neighbors. Through this education we'll learn to accept the truths of others. This learning is founded upon a few important virtues:

Humility helps us identify our own ignorance, faults, limitations, and biases. Humility opens our hearts and minds to the reality of others. It's a Christlike attitude that fosters spiritual maturity. Without it we'll never understand any reality other than our own, see different perspectives, or accept the truths of others.

The fear of the LORD is instruction in wisdom, and humility comes before honor. —**PROVERBS 15:33**

Imagination is an underappreciated virtue that provides us with the ability to pursue social justice. Without imagination, it's difficult to see the reality of others' experiences and viewpoints, especially when we can't rely on our own circumstances, experiences, cultures, and worldviews. By humbly learning about the oppression of those who have personally suffered from injustices, we can better imagine their reality.

> . . . that the God of our Lord Jesus Christ, the Father of glory, may give you the Spirit of wisdom and of revelation in the knowledge of him, having the eyes of your hearts enlightened, that you may know what is the hope to which he has called you. —**EPHESIANS 1:17-18**

Empathy is required to really see people for who they are—to understand what they've experienced, seen, felt, and thought. It allows us to accept their truth without being dismissive, combative, doubtful, invalidating, or hurtful. It helps us accept others wholly, fully affirming the reality of the injustices they have experienced and fully affirming the truth of who they are. Empathy believes, honors, respects, and loves. Empathy helps us see the very best in people as we adopt the vision of God, seeing others as beloved neighbors.

Do you know the golden rule? It's essentially a grand summation of empathy: "So whatever you wish that others would do to you, do also to them, for this is the Law and the Prophets" (Matthew 7:12).

Just as there are good virtues that help us gain wisdom, there are also destructive vices that prevent us from learning and connecting with others. Instead of nurturing goodness, these attitudes stymie the mind and war against education and wisdom.

Pride prevents us from learning because we assume we already know everything. Not only does it leave no room for new knowledge or growth, but it rebuffs even the most gentle offers of advice and instruction as an attack against oneself.

> When pride comes, then comes disgrace, but with the humble is wisdom. —**PROVERBS 11:2**

Fear prevents us from learning because we are scared of what we might learn, possibly revealing the depravity of ourselves and others. Sometimes we avoid the work of social justice because "the truth hurts." The reality that our police officers may hold racial prejudices, or that a local parish priest may be guilty of molesting children, or that our world isn't as nice and comfortable and convenient as we pretend it is can be difficult to accept. Social justice work will cause a lot of soul-searching, often revealing ugly truths in our past and current behaviors, ideas, and actions. This is scary, but necessary. It's daunting to get called out for our wrongdoings, face accountability, admit our mistakes, apologize, work towards making things right, experience confrontation, and willingly engage in the inevitable conflict of social chance. None of this is easy, but we do not need to fear it.

> God gave us a spirit not of fear but of power and love and self-control. —**2 TIMOTHY 1:7**

Hate refuses to learn from those it despises. Social justice teachers, educators, and activists may provide various avenues to learn, but hate works to erase the legitimacy of facts, truth, and honesty, and replaces it with a sheer feeling of walled resistance. Hate leads us to demonize the other. It slanders, attacks, and reinforces itself, seeking community with like-minded haters who fuel it. Hate spreads through lies and deception. Be a lover, not a hater.

Love is patient and kind; love does not envy or boast; it is not
arrogant or rude. It does not insist on its own way; it is not
irritable or resentful; it does not rejoice at wrongdoing, but
rejoices with the truth. Love bears all things, believes all things,
hopes all things, endures all things. —**1 CORINTHIANS 13:4-7**

In our eagerness to learn, we must respect the boundaries of others. We don't want to educate ourselves at the expense of compromising
someone else's emotional, spiritual, or physical well-being. This is especially difficult for victims of oppression, who are not only burdened
with injustice, but are often expected to repeatedly explain that burden
to others, reliving and experiencing that pain all over again. Learn, but
be gentle towards others, careful to honor their dignity and space.

Wisely steward the resources that may already be accessible to
you: books, podcasts, articles, classes, presentations, documentaries,
talks, interviews, and workshops. There are also an array of people who
willingly teach others, but in all circumstances, it's important to pay
others for their educational work, to recognize that our learning and
growth happens through the hard and valuable labor of others. They
deserve fair compensation. To take without giving back financially is
just another form of injustice.

Finally, once you've gained an important piece of knowledge, or
learned a particular truth that helps you love your neighbors more, it's
important to share it with others, and then act upon this wisdom in
your own life. Much of social justice work centers upon teaching others
and activism. It can be tempting to delegate this task, but it's our personal responsibility. The privilege of helping others pursue social justice
starts with us, and if we can change the heart and actions of just one
person, the world will move towards a better place.

MEDITATION

What's something new you've learned that's changed the way you view God and others over the span of your life? What is one area of social justice where you want to increase your knowledge? Is there an opportunity for you to help educate someone about a particular social justice issue?

PRAYER

Jesus the rabbi, my great teacher, please instruct me on how to love my neighbor as I would myself. Teach me to be a patient learner. Holy Spirit, please guide me; give me humility, strengthen my imagination, and bestow upon me the gift of empathy, so that I can truly see people. Forgive me for the times I've been prideful, fearful, and hateful, and I pray that I'll never be so foolish as to reject wisdom. Give me your eyes to see everyone for who they truly are, loved beyond compare. My hope is that I never diminish the divine humanity of others, but instead honor them and love them. God, give me the strength to learn, teach, and act.

Acquire Wisdom, Be a Scholar of Historical Truth

Let the wise hear and increase in learning, and the one who understands obtain guidance. —**PROVERBS 1:5**

The discerning heart seeks knowledge, but the mouth of a fool feeds on folly. —**PROVERBS 15:14 NIV**

An intelligent heart acquires knowledge, and the ear of the wise seeks knowledge. —**PROVERBS 18:15**

OPPRESSION RELIES on ignorance, apathy, and inaction. It thrives when we fail to recognize it and can't understand the oppressed—when we don't know them, their suffering, or even know what is causing it. When it is identified and understood, oppression then relies on our apathy. When we finally stir our passions against it, oppression then continues to survive through our inaction. Lastly, when we do act, oppression's final hope of existence cheers on our unwillingness to act sacrificially, because it assumes we'll not give up the time, energy, money, relationships, and hard work that's necessary to combat it.

Romans 5:7 observes that "one will scarcely die for a righteous person—though perhaps for a good person one would dare even to die." It then goes on to declare that God loves us so much that Jesus was willing to die for our sake. This is the sacrificial love required to participate in social justice. This radical love comes from the fact that God knows us.

God created us, and God's knowing us is a mystery far beyond our comprehension. But the psalmist declares, "O LORD, you have searched me and known me! You know when I sit down and when I rise up; you discern my thoughts from afar. You search out my path and my lying down and are acquainted with all my ways. Even before a word is on my tongue, behold, O LORD, you know it altogether" (Psalm 139:1-4). He says, "Your eyes saw my unformed substance; in your book were written, every one of them, the days that were formed for me, when as yet there was none of them" (v. 16). God loves us because God knows us.

Love requires *knowing*. How can we love the oppressed if we don't know them? How can we fight oppression if we don't recognize it? Social justice work thirsts for knowledge and understanding. As we pursue social justice, our pride, preconceptions, and narrow-mindedness have the opportunity to embrace humility, curiosity, and open-mindedness.

Social justice people are historians, listeners, readers, and observers. They are holders, bearers, and seekers of the truth, no matter how hard, brutal, or bloody those truths may be. Rather than closing our eyes and looking away, and rather than embracing the vacant comforts of ignorance, apathy, and denial, it is our purpose as followers of Jesus to look, to listen, to learn, to investigate . . . to *know*.

"Blessed is the one who finds wisdom,
    and the one who gets understanding,
for the gain from her is better than gain from silver

and her profit better than gold.
She is more precious than jewels,
    and nothing you desire can compare with her.
Long life is in her right hand;
    in her left hand are riches and honor.
Her ways are ways of pleasantness,
    and all her paths are peace." —**PROVERBS 3:13-17**

You are a collector of precious stories, a researcher who pores over source materials, a scholar who gathers information. You are a humble listener who treasures the words of a former enslaved person as they describe the working conditions of a sweatshop; or stories of a boy who grew up experiencing homelessness, or of a teenager who was forcibly conscripted as a soldier, or of a business professional who describes suffering through sexual harassment—different people from different places and circumstances whose voices you can choose to either accept or ignore. Their cries, whispers, pleas, and words of truth are often hidden or distorted by the distractions of our entertainment, economic, religious, social, and political noise—but they are there. At other times the pain and suffering of the oppressed is communicated directly to us without any distraction or barrier. What will you do with this?

Slavery. Genocide. War. Racism. Sexism. Ableism. Bigotry. Xenophobia. Hate. Greed. Corruption. Countries. Governments. Political Parties. Religions. Cultures. Economies. People, places, times, things, ideas, and events. Social justice connects us to them all. We can never know everything about everyone throughout all of time, but we can choose to know within our own time and place, within our own communities. Learn, listen, watch, read, know. Then act.

Avoid the populist narratives of the fearmongers and partisans, and task yourself with identifying your own prejudices and biases. Guard your heart and mind from the ever-tempting echo chambers of your own culture, upbringing, and socioeconomic circumstances. Give no quarter to revisionism or conspiracy theories, refute those who want to rewrite or erase the past and present—who attempt to manipulate the future.

You are a neighbor to the oppressed. Know them. Imagine their lives. Empathize with their hearts and minds. Experience their pain and suffering. Share in their hopes and dreams. Rejoice with them and weep with them. Amplify their voices. Love them.

It may be a normal day for you, but for others injustice in some form will forever alter their future. Things will happen today that will change history. A person my get arrested, a job may be lost, a piece of legislation could get passed by the government, or someone's parent may be deported. Do something today that will be an act of sacrificial love towards your neighbor. Remember that your life is meant to make the present and future better for the oppressed.

MEDITATION

The work of social justice inspires a willingness to learn. Below are some events worth discovering. If you already know what they are, find ones you don't. Otherwise, reflect on what happened and how people's live were changed. Prayerfully consider the real people impacted, and the circumstances that allowed these things to happen.

Louisville, Kentucky. August 6, 1855.

Mankato, Minnesota. December 26, 1862.

Marias River, Montana. January 23, 1870.

Los Angeles, California. October 24, 1871.

Čhaŋkpé Ópi Wakpála, present-day South Dakota. December 29, 1890.

Porvenir, Texas. January 28, 1918.

Elaine, Arkansas. September 30, 1919.

Tulsa, Oklahoma. May 31 and June 1, 1921.

Hiroshima, Japan. August 6, 1945.

Nagasaki, Japan. August 9, 1945.

Nogeun-ri, South Korea. July 26–29, 1950.

Iran. 1953.

Guatemala. 1954.

Sơn Mỹ, Vietnam. March 16, 1968.

Greenwich Village, New York. June 28, 1969.

New Orleans, Louisiana. June 24, 1973.

Persian Gulf. July 3, 1988.

Prince William Sound, Alaska. March 24, 1989.

Amiriyah neighborhood, Iraq. February 13, 1991.

Abu Ghraib prison, Iraq. 2003–2004.

Haditha, Iraq. November 19, 2005.

Al-Mahmudiyah, Iraq. March 12, 2006.

Granai, Afghanistan. May 4, 2009.

Kandahar Province, Afghanistan. March 11, 2012.

New York City. July 17, 2014.

Ferguson, Missouri. August 9, 2014.

Cleveland, Ohio. November 22, 2014.

North Charleston, South Carolina. April 4, 2015.

Orlando, Florida. June 12, 2016.

Baton Rouge, Louisiana. July 5, 2016.

St. Paul, Minnesota. July 6, 2016.

Tokhar, Syria. July 19, 2016.

Sacramento, California. March 18, 2018.

Louisville, Kentucky. March 18, 2018.

Minneapolis, Minnesota. May 25, 2020.

Washington D.C. January 6, 2021.

PRAYER

Dear God, forgive me for my ignorance. Teach me to know my neighbors. Teach me to love my neighbors.

DAY 31

Believe Survivors

The LORD works righteousness and justice for all who are oppressed.

—PSALM 103:6

INJUSTICE AND OPPRESSION prefer inaction, but social justice work asks us for a response. Justice wants something of us: To believe survivors, to help them, and to act in their defense. This is why ignoring—and denying the reality of—survivors is so enticing. Ignorance and apathy requires nothing of us. If we don't see, hear, or accept the truths of oppression, especially the uncomfortable truths, we can accept instead the deception that we have no responsibility in the matter.

Believing survivors is uncomfortable, but it's also a holy act of love. We may not want to deal with conflict, confrontation, law enforcement, or the process of accountability, but doing so is an act of love towards survivors. We may prefer the comfort and convenience of escapism, but for the sake of loving our neighbors we must advocate for others and *do something*.

Countless abuses, acts of violence, traumas, and deaths have happened because Christians were unwilling to believe survivors. They didn't believe children who were being abused. They didn't believe women who were being sexually assaulted. They didn't believe those who were brave enough to say something. Instead, they sided with their relatives, pastors, theologians, and leaders, unwilling to disrupt their own social lives and relationships, leaving suffering innocents in their wake.

This abandonment of survivors, and lack of accountability for perpetrators, is often spiritualized; we say things like, "It's biblical to confront this personally within the church rather than use outside law enforcement." We too often manipulate the concepts of forgiveness, unity, grace, mercy, moving forward, and "giving God the glory" in efforts to avoid accountability, hide crimes, invalidate victims, and make things go away. But any rationalization that protects the oppressors and denies justice to survivors is evil.

If you're a survivor, God sees you and loves you. God, who was mocked, tortured, and abused on the cross, abandoned by his friends and murdered in front of a jeering mob, is a God of justice. Justice *will* come, on this earth or in the world to come. Although the pain, suffering, and injustice may not yet have ended, the reality of the future kingdom of God is that God's judgment will enact justice. God is on your side.

Jesus was physically crucified by the Roman government, religious leaders, and citizenry of his day. They tried to suppress his voice and dismiss his proclamations, but when that failed, they killed him. In the end, some people believed Jesus, but many didn't. Oppressors can metaphorically crucify survivors socially, spiritually, and economically. They can threaten, cajole, slander, blackmail, and physically hurt survivors. Jesus sees, and knows, and empathizes with survivors, and so should we.

Silence, avoidance, and willful ignorance are complicity. Even participating in our religion can be an act of complicity if our faith is used as justification to oppress others. As people who follow Jesus, we are called by God to be on the side of survivors. So let's do our best to protect them and center them. May we help bring them justice. May we believe them. God help us.

MEDITATION

Has there ever been a time when you didn't believe someone who was telling the truth? Do you think victims are suppressed or prevented from being seen, heard, and believed? How and where do you see this?

PRAYER

God, give me the discernment to believe truth and the boldness to confront lies. I pray that I will defend the oppressed rather than blame them, honor them instead of vilify them, see them instead of ignore them. Forgive me for the times I failed them, and help me make things right.

DAY 32

Lament

Rejoice with those who rejoice, weep with those who weep.
—ROMANS 12:15

WHEN YOU LOVE someone, you share in their best and worst moments, in their rejoicing and in their weeping. Partaking in these intimate occasions and experiencing these deep times together is a holy and divine act of human solidarity. Healthy relationships will have many instances of lament, because anything great worth pursuing and obtaining—love, justice, peace, kindness, relationships—can be devastating when they are lost.

There's a holy power in lament, to weep as Jesus wept. Lament is one of the greatest and most profound expressions of love, because in it we embrace others with the empathy to understand, the vulnerability to share our deepest emotions, and the willingness to be present amid the darkest of circumstances. To lament is to engage in the hallowed act of communal grief. If we can't lament with our neighbors, do we really love them at all?

Following Jesus invites us to the important practice of lamenting. It's tempting to spiritualize joy in order to transform your religious experiences into a form of escapism, avoiding the truth of injustices, losses, pain, sorrow, and suffering. It's easier to avoid conflict, and many misinterpret faith as a state of being constantly happy; they treat sorrow and lament as something to avoid or eradicate. But forms of superficial "joy" refuse to embrace the reality of the world, and they forsake the reality of our weeping neighbors.

Few things are crueler or more inhumane than a church that refuses to weep with those who weep. God weeps with immigrants who are separated from their loved ones. God weeps with refugees who have lost everything to war. God weeps with the children who are enslaved and trafficked. God weeps with the abused, the sexually assaulted, and the victims of domestic violence. God weeps with those facing racism and xenophobia. God weeps with those experiencing bigotry. God weeps. God weeps with you, and welcomes us to weep with along with our neighbors.

Jesus wept. —**JOHN 11:35**

When the world looks to Christians for lament, this is an opportunity to embrace the suffering of others, to join in fellowship with those who are hurting. But too often Christians are silent, or apathetic, or even combative to the lament of others.

Scripture is full of laments. There's an entire book of the Bible entitled Lamentations. Roughly a third of all of the Psalms are forms of lament. Psalm 9:9 reflects the willingness of God to accept our laments, stating that "The LORD is a stronghold for the oppressed, a stronghold in times of trouble." Matthew 5:4 reiterates God's desire for us to lament, when Jesus exclaims "Blessed are those who mourn, for they shall be comforted." And Psalm 34:18 declares that "The LORD is near to the brokenhearted and saves the crushed in spirit." Scripture is full of lamentations because it reflects real life, and real life has moments of deep sorrow and pain.

Social justice asks us to lament, because justice cannot be passionately pursued until injustice is fully understood, and known, and felt. When you feel, see, and know the pain and suffering of your neighbors, you will lament.

Lamentations are happening all around us. The sorrows of the oppressed are being communicated, but are we listening? Social media posts, marches, protests, speeches, podcasts, books, interviews, the stories our coworkers tell us, the experiences our classmates suffer in front of us, the tears of our friends, all lamenting the injustices of the world.

Upon hearing these lamentations, will our response be to join in the lamenting, or will we silently turn away? When neighbors face oppression, they don't want or need our religious trivialities. To not lament is to not understand, to not empathize, to not have compassion, to not care, and to not love. When we lament with our neighbor we offer them our purest form of comfort, which doesn't rationalize, excuse, or shy away from the pain, but rather wholly embraces the reality of their being.

There are countless opportunities to lament, to love our neighbors: Bombings. Wars. Shooting. Murders. Racism. Bigotry. Today, lament with those who lament.

MEDITATION

What are some ways we can "weep with those who weep?" How can we become better at lamenting with our neighbors?

> How long, O Lord? Will you forget me forever?
> How long will you hide your face from me?
> How long must I take counsel in my soul
> and have sorrow in my heart all the day?
> How long shall my enemy be exalted over me?

Consider and answer me, O Lord my God;
  light up my eyes, lest I sleep the sleep of death,
lest my enemy say, "I have prevailed over him,"
  lest my foes rejoice because I am shaken.

But I have trusted in your steadfast love;
  my heart shall rejoice in your salvation.
I will sing to the Lord,
  because he has dealt bountifully with me.
—PSALM 13

Turn to me and be gracious to me,
  for I am lonely and afflicted.
The troubles of my heart are enlarged;
  bring me out of my distresses.
Consider my affliction and my trouble,
  and forgive all my sins.

Consider how many are my foes,
  and with what violent hatred they hate me.
Oh, guard my soul, and deliver me!
  Let me not be put to shame, for I take refuge in you.
May integrity and uprightness preserve me,
  for I wait for you. **—PSALM 25:16-21**

Blessed be the God and Father of our Lord Jesus Christ, the Father of mercies and God of all comfort, who comforts us in all our affliction, so that we may be able to comfort those who are in any affliction, with the comfort with which we ourselves are comforted by God. **—2 CORINTHIANS 1:3-4**

PRAYER

Dear God, may I learn to lament and to mourn with those who mourn, and to weep with those who weep. May my lamentations be a source of truth and honesty, and may they also provide great comfort and solidarity to my neighbors. Just as you are always by my side, may I similarly be there for those who are hurting. Help me to overcome any discomfort towards sharing my emotions with others, and give me the strength to embrace the pain and suffering of others as if it were my own. I pray for a sensitive heart that will be aware of my neighbors' troubles, and ask for an eagerness to be fully present with them.

DAY 33

Bearing Witness

A truthful witness saves lives. —**PROVERBS 14:25**

THE WORK OF social justice cannot be done unless injustice is first *seen*, and not until the victims are first acknowledged. To pursue social justice may force us into choosing between acceptance or denial, action or inaction, and we cannot face something we willfully choose to ignore.

Being a faithful witness means listening to survivors and believing them at their word without shaming, criticizing, or belittling. It means humbly accepting our own limitations and ignorance so we can clearly see and accept the truths of others. To identify and overcome our own biases, stereotypes, and presuppositions, we shouldn't force ourselves into only seeing what we want. Believing victims is not only a reflection of our trust, but also a symbol of our love. Being a truthful and honest witness tells the oppressed: We see you. We believe you. We love you.

Facing the truth and deciding to oppose injustice is hard, uncomfortable, and risky. It may mean confronting a friend about their abusive behavior, or reporting a coworker's racist remark, or talking to a family member about their xenophobic nationalism. Being a truthful witness leads us towards taking a stand and accepting the conflict and vulnerability necessary for doing the work of social justice. Recording a police interaction with your smartphone. Publicly disclosing the abuse of a well-liked personality. Reporting an incident of sexual harassment to HR. Seeking legal assistance and refusing to cover up injustices at your church, work, or school. The first step is hard, and might not be enough. It's often a matter of taking many steps. If nothing happens, press further, and harder, and continue to advocate, protect, and pursue justice for the sake of loving our neighbors.

Being a witness serves many important functions. It's a public act of solidarity where victims know that they're believed, loved, and worth fighting for. A witness upholds truth, which helps counteract propaganda, conspiracy theories, and historical revisionism. It reveals truth in the face of denialism. Injustice thrives upon lies, manipulation, and deceit, but an honest witness thwarts such evils. Sincere witnesses also serve to influence public sentiment, and honesty, validity, and accuracy legitimize social justice causes while simultaneously destroying unjust ones.

Standing between the perpetrators of oppression and the victims are numerous people, agendas, and systems, and sometimes all it takes for justice to happen is for one person to courageously rise up and truthfully take a stand. Tyranny assumes most will be too uncomfortable, afraid, busy, or distracted. Are we?

As Christians, we've often failed at being witnesses. Throughout history we saw oppression but mostly did nothing. Racism, sexism, and bigotry were met with either complicity or silence. Because of this, racist, sexist, and bigoted movements found a home in churches across the United States, and instead of combating injustice, Christianity became one of its largest producers. Sadly, many times we as Christians weren't willing to fight oppression. Because of this, a political movement of millions would embrace Christian nationalism, White supremacy, and xenophobia. A patriarchal system objectified, oppressed, and shamed women, and rampant misogyny and sexual abuse permeated Christian communities. LGBTQIA+ individuals faced bigoted hate from all sectors of Christianity, and the emotional and physical trauma was so widespread that the damage is still unfolding. As Christians, we must boldly be a witness and condemn oppression in all its forms. But even as injustices continue today, we still struggle to bear witness. Too many of us see oppression but do nothing. The consequence of such inaction is the loss of human dignity and life.

We must be willing to be a witness. The labor of social justice—like following Christ—is a marathon. It can be grueling, difficult, and exhausting, but by participating in social justice work we bear one another's burdens: the burdens of injustice, inequity, and oppression. We do this because of love, and love doesn't give up easily. Press on, sojourner, and keep up the good fight.

MEDITATION

I have fought the good fight, I have finished the race, I have kept the faith. —**2 TIMOTHY 4:7**

Whoever speaks the truth gives honest evidence, but a false witness utters deceit. —**PROVERBS 12:17**

Have you witnessed injustice within your life? How can you be a public witness against injustice? Do you see any oppression or injustice that's being rationalized or rejected by society?

PRAYER

God, give me the strength and courage to be a witness. May I be a truth-bearer, no matter how uncomfortable or inconvenient the truth may be. Give me eyes to see and ears to hear the cries of the oppressed. Allow me to see and feel the pain of my neighbors. Then give me the courage to pursue justice. May I never prefer to escape into the comfort of ignorance and avoidance. Please send your spirit to lead me to the forefront of loving the world around me.

DAY 34

‹——⟩

Religious Bias

When justice is done, it is a joy to the righteous but terror to
evildoers. —**PROVERBS 21:15**

TRUTH AND HONESTY reflect the life and character of Jesus, but
even though they're Christian virtues, we still tell lies and exhibit dishonest behavior. Being a Christian doesn't guarantee truth or honesty. Non-
Christians can be just as truthful and honest as people or organizations
that identify as being Christian—often even more so. Truth and honesty
are universal attributes that can be accepted and practiced by anyone. All
truth is God's truth, but we discover many truths beyond the realm of
the Bible, churches, and our own faith communities. Our knowledge of
math, science, art, entertainment, professional skills, and all sorts of talents, information, abilities, and insights is obtained through many sources outside of our religious practices. Similarly, although social justice is a
Christian virtue that's rooted in the life of Jesus, it can also be practiced
and facilitated *better* by non-Christians, and we must gain knowledge,
wisdom, and proficiency in it by going beyond the Christian world.

If social justice is Christianized to look exactly like our religion, it will blind us to our religion's own injustices. It will enable oppression rather than stop it. There are deep spiritual inspirations for social justice, and strong theological foundations for its practice, but social justice also manifests itself best when facilitated with a cool temperament and pragmatic approach. We can celebrate the divine truth of social justice by emphasizing our faith, but this must never come at the expense of also being practical and utilitarian. Social justice work invites us to go beyond the influence of our religious biases and spiritual zeal in order to better analyze, accept hard facts, and do the right thing. Doing this is especially difficult when the injustice we must confront involves someone we love—a pastor, a friend, or family member.

Historically, we as Christians have committed countless injustices and been guilty of many forms of oppression. Clergy abuse of minors, sexism, racism, and various forms of violence have all been done by the church (and are still happening today), and we've failed at fulfilling our own self-proclaimed social justice ideals. We cannot police ourselves. This is why social justice must be outside of our control and free from the constraints of our own—and our faith community's—selfish desires, wishes, and limited perceptions. The work of social justice is shared as a communal endeavor, accepted and practiced as a universal truth by both Christians and non-Christians alike. So let's humbly welcome the invitation to learn from others, from those who don't share our preferred theology, denomination, or religion.

MEDITATION

By confronting injustice within Christianity, we are doing a good and holy work. Proverbs 21:3 states that "To do righteousness and justice is more acceptable to the LORD than sacrifice." Social justice is an act of worship.

Have you or someone you know ever been hurt by the church? What are some historical examples of churches or Christians who have oppressed others? How can we confront oppression being done by our own religion?

PRAYER

God, forgive me for co-opting my religion and failing to uphold justice within my own faith communities. Give me the courage and integrity to stop oppression, whether it's being done by a stranger or by my very own pastor. May I not be fooled into believing I'm immune to being unjust or oppressive just because I identify with you. Help me repent from my complicity, my apathy, and my ignorance. I'm sorry for my hypocrisy, and for all the times I judged others yet remained prideful in my self-righteousness. Humble me.

Taking God's Name in Vain

"You shall not take the name of the LORD your God in vain, for the LORD will not hold him guiltless who takes his name in vain."

—EXODUS 20:7

TAKING GOD'S NAME in vain is when the Christian religion is used for personal, political, and economic gain, or when it's weaponized to oppress others.

Jesus rarely got angry, but when he did, it was because people were misusing and abusing religion—they were taking God's name in vain. When Jesus cleared the money changers from the temple courts by furiously driving them out in a fit of rage, he was upset because the temple was being exploited to turn a profit under the flimsy premise of spirituality and holiness. Jesus was also livid when the Pharisees hypocritically didn't reflect the godliness they themselves preached. Jesus chastised them by saying, "So for the sake of your tradition you have made void the word of God. You hypocrites! Well did Isaiah prophesy of you, when he said: 'This people honors me with their lips, but their heart is far from me: in vain do they worship me, teaching as doctrines the commandments of men'" (Matthew 15:6-9).

We're meant to exude grace, mercy, patience, and love. But when we don't extend these gifts to others—the same gifts Christ has generously bestowed to us—we're taking God's name in vain. If we assume we're given undeserved grace yet use Christianity as an excuse to not extend grace within our justice systems, within the very society where we live and breathe, we're taking God's name in vain. If we claim our citizenship in heaven is due to God's mercy towards us, yet argue against extended citizenship to immigrants applying for citizenship within our own country, we're taking God's name in vain. If we assume Christ defends us and protects us, yet we use Christianity to avoid doing the same for refugees, the poor, the oppressed, and anyone in need, we're taking God's name in vain.

Hypocrisy. Profiteering. Greed. Fear. Hate. Racism. Xenophobia. Bigotry. When Christianity is used to facilitate these things, God's name is being used in vain. If you're tired of a religion and spirituality that takes God's name in vain, start the work of social justice. The endeavors of social justice are the opposite of taking God's name in vain because they're selfless acts of love towards others. This love transcends denominations and doctrines, goes beyond theological beliefs or partisan opinions, and isn't motivated by money, religion, or politics. It's a love that doesn't ask for a specific form of baptism, request a donation, expect attendance at a church, or hope for a conversion.

"Not everyone who says to me, 'Lord, Lord,' will enter the kingdom of heaven, but the one who does the will of my Father who is in heaven. On that day many will say to me, 'Lord, Lord, did we not prophesy in your name, and cast out demons in your name, and do many mighty works in your name?' And then will I declare to them, 'I never knew you; depart from me, you workers of lawlessness.'" —**MATTHEW 7:21-23**

MEDITATION

Have you ever experienced a time when Christianity was misused for personal gain, hate, abuse, or oppression? What are some moments you've experienced when Christianity failed you or someone you love? How can you use your faith to work for social justice instead of against it?

PRAYER

Dear God, please forgive us for the times we've misused our faith to hate and oppress our neighbors. May we recognize that Christianity is ultimately about loving you and loving our neighbors—loving all of humanity. May we stop using religion to control people or gain power, but instead emulate Jesus to love others to the very best of our ability.

DAY 36

Truth-Bearers

But if anyone has the world's goods and sees his brother in need,
yet closes his heart against him, how does God's love abide in him?
Little children, let us not love in word or talk but in deed
and in truth. —**1 JOHN 3:17-18**

SOCIAL JUSTICE work loves in deed and in truth. Rather than
being too theologically lofty, or too distracted by spiritualized worship,
or too noisy with religious talk and posturing, the social justice–mind-
ed Christian acts and serves as a practical realist. We direct the love of
God back to where it's supposed to go: people. While our church may
work on lavish productions, having a great coffee bar, and tech-sav-
vy marketing campaigns, we serve as a blunt reminder, guiding our
Christian community so that it can effectively carry out God's love for
the oppressed.

The path of social justice asks people to decide whether they prefer
truth or ignorant bliss. It upholds truth as an attainable and palpable
reality that can be discovered and obtained. Truth is often ugly, and it

can lead us to places of discomfort and pain. We discover that our loved ones are abusers, or that our country isn't as innocent as we thought it was, or find out that a friend assaulted someone. Truth is confrontational and messy, and it often nudges us to either action or inaction.

The enemies of truth are, in no particular order: propaganda, partisan rhetoric, conspiracy theories, revisionism, nationalism, denial, nondisclosure agreements, marketing and PR firms, silence, hate, fear, curated social media platforms, Satan, and grandparents who watch their grandkids during any form of competition.

The allies of truth are, in no particular order: vulnerability, honesty, humility, curiosity, courage, imagination, patience, research, reason, logic, evidence, knowledge, wisdom, Jesus, and an angry spouse.

The pursuit of social justice tethers Christianity to the world around it. It serves to free us from our ignorance and complacency, and protects us from the tendency towards spiritual escapism. We are to be truth-bearers because God values truth and reality over religious decorum. God would rather we faithfully address the systemic racism, xenophobia, and partisan hate within our communities than attend church services that avoid the realities of injustice. The truth is that injustice is real, and oppression is real . . . and often pervasive.

God hates faith that doesn't provide any realistic love, truthful love, to the people around it, and the following verses prove it:

> They profess to know God, but they deny him by their works. They are detestable, disobedient, unfit for any good work.
> **—TITUS 1:16**

> What good is it, my brothers, if someone says he has faith but does not have works? Can that faith save him? If a brother or sister is poorly clothed and lacking in daily food, and one of you says to them, "Go in peace, be warmed and filled," without giving

them the things needed for the body, what good is that? So also faith by itself, if it does not have works, is dead. —**JAMES 2:14-17**

"Beware of false prophets, who come to you in sheep's clothing but inwardly are ravenous wolves. You will recognize them by their fruits. Are grapes gathered from thornbushes, or figs from thistles? So, every healthy tree bears good fruit, but the diseased tree bears bad fruit. A healthy tree cannot bear bad fruit, nor can a diseased tree bear good fruit. Every tree that does not bear good fruit is cut down and thrown into the fire. Thus you will recognize them by their fruits.

"Not everyone who says to me, 'Lord, Lord,' will enter the kingdom of heaven, but the one who does the will of my Father who is in heaven. On that day many will say to me, 'Lord, Lord, did we not prophesy in your name, and cast out demons in your name, and do many mighty works in your name?' And then will I declare to them, 'I never knew you; depart from me, you workers of lawlessness.' —**MATTHEW 7:15-23**

Social justice work is the good fruit God seeks to find within us, a practical love that engages the real world and those in need. The practice of social justice is good work that's made up of *good works*, fueled by our faith in Jesus, which eventually will bear good fruit. When we participate in the action of social justice, God will be glorified and honor our work.

Always remember that Christianity is rooted in social justice for the benefit of others—for the love of our neighbors. Christianity is not a religion meant to disconnect from the world, but rather to fully embrace the realness happening in our world.

MEDITATION

How are Christians being either a truthful or a dishonest witness within today's society? What are some practical things you can do to publicly be a truthful witness regarding social justice? Has there ever been a time when admitting or revealing the truth was too hard for you?

PRAYER

God, may I be an ambassador of truth. I want to learn truth, know truth, speak truth, and spread truth. I want to be truthful. Open my mind to the truth of others, to the truth of those being oppressed and facing injustice. Jesus, your life and actions and words are true, which is why I know social justice is the pursuit of truth. May I have the strength to accept truth and to be honest with both myself and others.

Social Justice as a Christian Way of Life

Whoever says "I know him" but does not keep his commandments is a liar, and the truth is not in him. —**1 JOHN 2:4**

Despite the fact that the Bible documents Jesus only presenting a few public sermons, much of our faith tradition has become structured around the attendance of a weekly sermon presented by a church leader. Although a large percentage of our Christian existence is made up listening to teachings, Jesus only had one talk that was labeled a sermon: the Sermon on the Mount. It's within the middle of this Sermon on the Mount that Jesus declares ". . . whatever you wish that others would do to you, do also to them, for this is the Law and the Prophets" (Matthew 7:12). The great irony of our modern Christian practices is that we spend a significant amount of our time participating in the discipline of listening to sermons, upon which we learn that Jesus spent a significant amount of his time facilitating acts of social justice.

We've transformed Christianity into a set of beliefs rather than a state of being. Discipleship has become a matter of theological indoctrination, denominational certification, and philosophical training rather than a way of loving our neighbors.

Learning about the way Jesus' disciples healed people, met new people, interacted with the community, broke social barriers, and ministered to the sick is a good thing. But instead of emulating Jesus' life through the work of social justice, it's tempting to just study it, memorize it, and obsess over it. We can even ignore Jesus and delve into parts of the Bible as a distraction, focusing on specific themes, verses, possible interpretations that better satisfy our selfish desires.

It's through the pretense of spiritual habits that we can practice Christianity without actually being Christlike. When we hide within the comforts of our self-made religion we diminish our ability to effectively love our neighbors. If we're not careful, we can become experts at pretending to be righteous while not following Jesus at all.

Jesus uses frightening illustrations to emphasize the importance of going beyond just religious beliefs. In Matthew chapter 25 he says:

"When the Son of Man comes in his glory, and all the angels with him, then he will sit on his glorious throne. Before him will be gathered all the nations, and he will separate people one from another as a shepherd separates the sheep from the goats. And he will place the sheep on his right, but the goats on the left. Then the King will say to those on his right, 'Come, you who are blessed by my Father, inherit the kingdom prepared for you from the foundation of the world. For I was hungry and you gave me food, I was thirsty and you gave me drink, I was a stranger and you welcomed me, I was naked and you clothed me, I was sick and you visited me, I was in prison and you came to me.' Then the righteous will answer him, saying, 'Lord, when did we see you hungry and feed you, or thirsty and give you drink? And when did we see you a stranger and welcome you, or naked and clothe you? And when did we see you sick or in prison and visit you?' And the King will answer them, 'Truly, I say to you, as you did it to one of the least of these my brothers, you did it to me.'

"Then he will say to those on his left, 'Depart from me, you cursed, into the eternal fire prepared for the devil and his angels. For I was hungry and you gave me no food, I was thirsty and you gave me no drink, I was a stranger and you did not welcome me, naked and you did not clothe me, sick and in prison and you did not visit me.' Then they also will answer, saying, 'Lord, when did we see you hungry or thirsty or a stranger or naked or sick or in prison, and did not minister to you?' Then he will answer them, saying, 'Truly, I say to you, as you did not do it to one of the least of these, you did not do it to me.' And these will go away into eternal punishment, but the righteous into eternal life.

—MATTHEW 25:31-46

Here, in the harshest of tones, Jesus describes salvation as a matter of how we love (or don't love) others, of how we help "the least of these." Now compare this with perhaps the most oft-quoted verse in all of the Bible (John 3:16), which says, "For God so loved the world, that he gave his only Son, that whoever believes in him should not perish but have eternal life." I think Christians prefer John 3:16 because it's the most comforting path to salvation: a mere belief. But what if this "whoever believes in him" that's referenced in John 3:16 means something else entirely? What if it assumes the reader understands and follows what Jesus repeatedly claims the gospel actually is? What if salvation is what Christ models continuously throughout his entire life and ministry, that to believe in God means loving your neighbor?

Social justice is a state of being where our beliefs and convictions are continuously lived out through a love for others. "Do unto others" is our motto not just because it's the core of what social justice is, but because it's the very heart of God.

MEDITATION

How can we transform our beliefs about loving our neighbor into practical action steps? List a few simple things you can do to love your neighbor, then try to do them.

PRAYER

God, help me never to let my religion get in the way of loving my neighbor. I believe in loving my neighbor, but give me the bravery and courage to actually manifest those beliefs in real and practical ways.

DAY 38

Kindness and Humility

What does the LORD require of you but to do justice, and to love
kindness, and to walk humbly with your God? —**MICAH 6:8**

KINDNESS AND HUMILITY allow us to acknowledge the dignity
and worth of another human being. They're a few of the most basic forms
of love. Kindness and humility are words and actions towards someone
that are willfully positive and selflessly given for the benefit of another.

Social justice work is relational by nature, and is best employed
by having an attitude of kindness and humility. Social justice work is
learned through the humble posture of a student who recognizes one's
own limitations, ignorance, and faults, while simultaneously honoring
the expertise, abilities, and wisdom of others. Social justice work humbly
accepts one's own failures and mistakes, and willingly apologizes and tries
to do better. Social justice work must be kind, both to oneself and others,
because without kindness love cannot prevail. Social justice work abides
by the principles found in Ephesians, "Be kind to one another, tender-
hearted, forgiving one another, as God in Christ forgave you" (Ephesians

4:32), and also the one found in Peter, "Above all, keep loving one another earnestly, since love covers a multitude of sins" (1 Peter 4:8).

This humility and kindness isn't passive or superficial. It's not a condescending superiority complex that accepts others for the sake of being politically correct. It's not fake smiles, or politely giving advice, or cheap charity, or simply being nice. No, this kindness and humility is deep and bold, and it constantly centers others above one's own self. It promotes others, cares for others, respects others, and loves others.

Be kind and show humility towards others. The Bible says that "If you are kind only to your friends, how are you different from anyone else?" (Matthew 5:47 NLT). Do you show kindness and humility towards the poor, the incarcerated, immigrants, refugees, the sick, the homeless, the disabled, to those who identify with different beliefs, religions, sexual and gender orientations, cultures, and ethnicities other than your own?

Being kind and humble doesn't require always being happy or never being angry. It doesn't mean that victims of oppression must meet unrealistic expectations of morality, kindness, and humility in order to deserve justice. It simply means we must strive to be like Jesus.

And Jesus did get angry. Christ furiously cleared the moneychangers out of the temple courts and angrily denounced the hypocrisy of the religious leaders. He did this because he cared for others, but also because both instances were cases of injustice. In the temple, religion was being used as a form of corrupt profiteering. And Jesus rebukes the religious hypocrites by saying, "But you have neglected the more important matters of the law—justice, mercy and faithfulness" (Matthew 23:23 NIV).

Anger isn't often associated with kindness, but by definition being considerate is part of kindness. If we don't get angry when we witness corruption, injustice, inequity, and cruelty being directed towards our neighbors, we aren't considering them, and therefore aren't being kind. Anger is an appropriate response because we're considering the injustice and oppression that's happening to others.

When kindness, consideration, and humility are lacking, the void is filled with hatred and pride, which fuels and ignites injustices. Social justice work must never devolve into social cruelty or social shaming. Many people have struggled with social justice not because they lacked knowledge, ability, passion, or the necessary resources to create change, but because they lacked kindness and humility. Contrarily, many have succeeded with social justice work because their humility and kindness were a force that overcame oppression. Social justice work embraces the heart of God, loving others just as Jesus loves us.

MEDITATION

Love is patient and kind; love does not envy or boast; it is not arrogant or rude. It does not insist on its own way; it is not irritable or resentful; it does not rejoice at wrongdoing, but rejoices with the truth. Love bears all things, believes all things, hopes all things, endures all things. —**1 CORINTHIANS 13:4-7**

Let each of you look not only to his own interests, but also to the interests of others. —**PHILIPPIANS 2:4**

What's the difference between real kindness and superficial kindness? How can you be more humble in the process of pursuing social justice?

PRAYER

God, I claim this truth: "Whoever pursues righteousness and kindness will find life, righteousness, and honor" (Proverbs 21:21). And may I always remember that "When pride comes, then comes disgrace, but with the humble is wisdom" (Proverbs 11:2). Jesus, help me to be more like you. I want to be kind, and humble, and considerate of others. I pray that I'll look out for my neighbor's best interests, so that I may love my neighbors in the same way that you love me.

DAY 39

Judge Not

"Judge not, that you be not judged." —**MATTHEW 7:1**

AS CHRISTIANS, we're often guilty of judgmentalism. Partisan Christianity relies on prideful and selfish judgmentalism because it relies upon "us vs. them" narratives. Christians vs. non-Christians. Those who go to heaven vs. those who go to hell. Catholics vs. Protestants. Republican vs. Democrat Christians. Pro-choice vs. pro-life Christians. Affirming vs. non-affirming Christians. American vs. non-American Christians. Countless subgroups splinter into how someone is viewed as either a good Christian, a bad Christian, or not a Christian at all. These forms of judging people under the guise of religion, morality, and salvation are detestable human-made hierarchical structures that ignore God's inclusive love of everyone.

Social justice work cannot be judgmental because being so excludes love. We may not be able to completely relate to, or perfectly understand, the victims of oppression. But we can try. Their circumstances and experiences may be unfamiliar to us, but this doesn't mean we can't empathize with victims or are incapable of some understanding.

It could be that we'll never be able to fully comprehend or experience the depth of pain, suffering, and trauma of others. But this shouldn't prevent us from loving them and fighting for justice on their behalf.

Humanity is complex, and each person feels, reacts, and exists differently when faced with oppression. There's no one-size-fits-all model way of battling, surviving, or processing injustice. We don't have a homogeneous method of doing social justice work. It's a pursuit that's constantly changing, evolving, and unique for each person, place, and circumstance. Yes, there are overarching injustices and forms of oppression that need to be ended. There are even common strategies to combat them. But how this is done, or why, or who gets to do it—the timing of it, the methods, processes, and ways the details happen—are often a matter of personal opinion and disagreement.

To accept complexity is hard work. Complexity takes time, humility, and patience. Those who reject complexity, or fail to see another's perspective, embrace judgmentalism. Being judgmental prevents learning, growth, and maturity. It's the prideful embrace of believing one is right no matter what, even when wrong. Judgmentalism prefers personal narratives and experiences over the truth of others, and it discards any worldview, experience, and logic outside of one's own. It cannot *see* other people, because it cannot understand other people's lives, lives that consist of different truths, experiences, beliefs, and opinions.

Judgmentalism thwarts progress by reverting to fundamentalism, because it only views the world through a narrow perspective. Being judgmental prevents the mind from accepting different possibilities, or even regarding the truths of others. Because of this, the realities of others, of those who are oppressed and experiencing injustice, are denied. Proverbs 18:2 exclaims that "a fool takes no pleasure in understanding, but only in expressing his opinion." Matthew 7:1-2 also warns against the severity of judging others by declaring, "Judge not, that you be not judged. For with the judgment you pronounce you will be judged, and with the measure you use it will be measured to you." God clearly doesn't want us judging and making assumptions about others.

Judgmental attitudes lead to policing victims on how they should react to injustice, berating them for how they respond to oppression, preaching about "proper" methods of dealing with abuse, or debating how victims might have avoided their suffering or could have done something different. "They wouldn't be poor if only they worked harder," "If they had only followed what the police officer said," and "What kind of parent would try to bring their child illegally into another country?!" are all examples of judgmentalism. Judgmentalism is dismissive of people, and centers ourselves over our neighbors. Be humble. Empathize. Lament. Learn. And for the sake of God, don't judge.

MEDITATION

Has someone ever misjudged you? Have you ever misjudged a situation or person?

> Judge not, and you will not be judged; condemn not, and you will not be condemned; forgive, and you will be forgiven. —**LUKE 6:37**

> "Therefore you have no excuse, O man, every one of you who judges. For in passing judgment on another you condemn yourself, because you, the judge, practice the very same things. We know that the judgment of God rightly falls on those who practice such things. Do you suppose, O man—you who judge those who practice such things and yet do them yourself—that you will escape the judgment of God?" —**ROMANS 2:1-3**

PRAYER

Dear God, I pray that I won't self-righteously judge others or presume to understand experiences I've never experienced, people I've never met, and circumstances I've never lived through. I ask for humility and compassion, and please fill me with love and mercy.

Unstained from the World

Religion that is pure and undefiled before God the Father, is this:
to visit orphans and widows in their affliction, and to keep oneself
unstained from the world. —**JAMES 1:27**

SOCIAL JUSTICE work is divine by nature. It's unnatural to the world we live in. Social justice work, like all holy pursuits, will be met with unholy oppositions that will manifest themselves in both mundane and extraordinary forms. They will prey upon your physical, intellectual, emotional, and spiritual being. Any endeavor that pursues the ideals of Jesus—to visit orphans and widows and those experiencing affliction—will face opposition.

To have a lucrative career. To be safe. To play it safe, and never have to fear making a mistake. To acquire fame and fortune, or spend your time pursuing it. To travel. To enjoy yourself. To invest in your family. To make wise financial choices. To not waste time and energy. To protect oneself from shame, fear, and conflict. These aren't bad things, but good things often serve as the best excuses to not pursue justice.

God has purposed your life to bring justice, love, and mercy to humanity. Despite any misgivings you have about social justice work, please realize that you are worthy to do this important undertaking. Although you may not believe in yourself, God trusts you, and you are vital to the mission of justice.

To be unstained from the world, one must not let the world dictate the terms that are meant to be ordained by God. To let our lives be ordered by unholy callings, desires, and actions is to engage in idolatry. Jesus proclaims that "if you were of the world, the world would love you as its own; but because you are not of the world, but I chose you out of the world, therefore the world hates you" (John 15:19). You will be hated for the sake of pursuing social justice.

This doesn't mean embracing an anti-world abhorrence of everything secular. Being unstained from the world doesn't require us to live a minimalist life of monasticism, but it does necessitate orienting ourselves to the goals and desires of God, which are to love our neighbors.

To love our neighbors and do social justice work is to be unstained from the world. Your friends and family may hate it. Your church may hate it. Your government will hate it. Your job may hate it. Your school may hate it. There are many people, places, and things that will hate it, but God isn't one of them. Because God loves social justice work.

MEDITATION

Do not be conformed to this world, but be transformed by the renewal of your mind, that by testing you may discern what is the will of God, what is good and acceptable and perfect.

—ROMANS 12:2

How does social justice contradict or conform to the expectations of your family, your friends, your church, your job, your society? When has the work of social justice been a burden to you or someone else?

PRAYER

Holy God, give me the grit to faithfully pursue social justice. May I do good for your kingdom rather than for my own personal gain. When I'm tempted by fame, riches, or power, may I take the path less traveled. Help me to love you and love my neighbors even when it is inconvenient. And when I feel tired, embarrassed, or scared, empower me to do the right thing for the sake of helping others.

DAY 41

Money and Sacrifice

If among you, one of your brothers should become poor, in any of your towns within your land that the LORD your God is giving you, you shall not harden your heart or shut your hand against your poor brother, but you shall open your hand to him and lend him sufficient for his need, whatever it may be. Take care lest there be an unworthy thought in your heart and you say, "The seventh year, the year of release is near," and your eye look grudgingly on your poor brother, and you give him nothing, and he cry to the LORD against you, and you be guilty of sin. You shall give to him freely, and your heart shall not be grudging when you give to him, because for this the LORD your God will bless you in all your work and in all that you undertake. For there will never cease to be poor in the land. Therefore I command you, "You shall open wide your hand to your brother, to the needy and to the poor, in your land." —**DEUTERONOMY 15:7-11**

THE DIFFERENCE BETWEEN superficial rhetoric and selfless love is one's willingness to sacrifice. Social justice—loving your neighbor, and loving God—asks us to give. To give our time, our energy, our money, and maybe even our life. In societies that idolize wealth and glorify individualistic consumerism, giving up our wealth to help others, or prioritizing others more than prioritizing obtaining wealth, can be seen as almost profane. In fact, a common insult for people engaged in social justice work often sounds something like this: "Don't these people have jobs? If they worked they wouldn't have all of this spare time!" The idea that people could actually value other people—could actually love their neighbor—more than functioning within a consumer role is often seeing as a radical, even illogical value.

Social justice work protects people over property, defends people more than possessions, values people more than wealth, and would rather gain the well-being of the oppressed than obtain all the riches that injustice would otherwise offer. Social justice work routinely avoids carnal temptations for the sake of others. It works for a humane society for all instead of a booming economy for a few, prefers an affordable home for the poor rather than a mansion for oneself, and it makes a common habit of leaving the ninety-nine to save the one. Social justice work is terribly inefficient, extraordinarily costly, and the very antithesis to fame and fortune.

Jesus once encountered a rich young ruler. This man was devout, a lifelong adherent to the religious teachings, yet after interacting with Jesus the rich man went away dejected, because Jesus asked him to sell all of his possessions and give the resulting profits to the poor. Jesus promised that doing so would ensure greater riches for the man within the kingdom of God. But the man went away heartbroken because he knew the great value of his possessions and didn't want to lose them. Who can blame this person? He's the biblical version of a modern capitalist. This person might have worked hard to acquire his wealth, and his faith community could have praised him for being a good steward of his money and for making wise investments. He probably led the congregation's financial management self-help classes. Jesus offers a less flattering description of the man though, saying, "It is easier for a camel to go through the eye of a needle than for a rich person to enter the kingdom of God" (Mark 10:25).

> "No one can serve two masters, for either he will hate the one and love the other, or he will be devoted to the one and despise the other. You cannot serve God and money." —**MATTHEW 6:24**

This proclamation by Christ is an indictment against any government, business, organization, society, church, or individual that has ever committed injustice for the sake of money. Injustice is often rooted in the love of money, where the quest for wealth overcomes any sense of morality, equity, and even humanity.

Military invasions, coup d'états, genocides, enslavements, land robberies, segregation, redlining, insurance scams, union busting, subpar working conditions, child labor, private prisons, law enforcement, insurance scams, corporate lobbyists, corrupt politicians, lost benefits, market crashes, the lack of a living wage, unjust laws, expensive healthcare, predatory loans, usury interest rates, and all of the fine print, loopholes, and legal threats of extortive litigation. All of this pain, suffering, and injustice often occurs because of a love of money.

It's been said that budgets are moral documents, and in a world where much of our lives are spent obtaining money, how we spend it reflects our heart's passions. Unfortunately, we're not great at being sacrificially giving. We prefer minimal giving, status quo giving, pretending-to-be-generous giving. Our consumeristic tendencies rationalize that we need "our" money for an emergency, for retirement, or for new clothes.

The world runs on money. It's why most of us get up in the morning, to get ready for work, to go do our jobs. But the kingdom of God runs on love. When we have a kingdom of God mindset we pursue social justice work with the same professionalism and tenacity that we pursue money. We do this because at some point in our life, we realized one of the most important truths that God has been trying to tell humanity for forever: people are more valuable than money. People are divinely made by God, created in God's image, and loved by God. It's a wonderful truth that you, me, and everyone else is loved by God. In the Bible, the most crucial part of the entire story is when God sends his only son Jesus to sacrifice himself on the cross. God did this because God loves us. God didn't do this for the love of money, or wealth, or power, or any country, but for us—humanity.

Social justice work understands that people are of divine worth, and this revelation changes one's entire worldview. Doing social justice work still may mean that we have jobs, garner a salary, go to school, engage in entertainment, and even appear to live normal lives, but we must also understand that we have a holy mandate that supersedes everything: to love our neighbors.

The goals, decisions, and actions of social justice work should be guided by this mantra: Do whatever is the most loving. Unlike businesses that are driven by profits, or factories that are run on efficiency, or consumers who are obsessed with money and costs, Christians passionate about social justice should be ultimately motivated by love.

Just because love is the primary motivation for social justice work doesn't negate the importance of money. Many social justice causes advocate for more money. Income inequality due to sexism, racism, bigotry, reparations, and a livable wage are all social justice issues that revolve around money. Money is also needed for healthcare, food, education, housing, and other resources that people need in order to live a good, safe, and fulfilling life. In most cases, the money needed for social justice work exists but is either hoarded, withheld, or "budgeted" to benefit the wealthiest and most powerful. For example, in America, hundreds of billions of dollars are used for the military, corporate subsidies, and tax breaks for the richest businesses and citizens, while only a fraction of the economic resources are diverted to help our neighbors in need.

Social justice work uses, allocates, and asks for money because of a love for others. We don't seek money out of greed or because we think it's more powerful than love, but rather we see it as a practical manifestation of our love. We want our neighbors to be safe, to have a home, livable wage, proper healthcare, a good education, and a life that's valuable and worthwhile because people are divinely valuable and of unsurpassable worth—and this takes money. Often, this requires our money.

The rich young ruler whom Jesus talks with in the Bible represents many of us today. We're faithful churchgoers who attend budgeting classes and go through financial self-help programs, and we rigorously strive to accrue money, gain wealth, and follow all of God's commands . . . well, almost all of them.

Just as Jesus challenged the rich young ruler to sell his possessions and give to the poor, God challenges us to look at our own bank statements and asks us to sacrificially give to the poor, and also give to the refugee, the immigrant, the homeless, the sick, the underpaid, the hungry, and oppressed, and anyone who could be better loved through our financial sacrifice.

MEDITATION

As for the rich in this present age, charge them not to be haughty, nor to set their hopes on the uncertainty of riches, but on God, who richly provides us with everything to enjoy. They are to do good, to be rich in good works, to be generous and ready to share, thus storing up treasure for themselves as a good foundation for the future, so that they may take hold of that which is truly life.

—1 TIMOTHY 6:17-19

This is that which is truly life: "to do good, to be rich in good works, to be generous and ready to share."

Obviously, it's not a mandate that every Christian sell all of their possessions, but how can you practice being more generous? How does money influence or control your life? Look over your finances: is there room to give to those in need?

PRAYER
Recite the Lord's Prayer:

Our Father which art in heaven, Hallowed be thy name.
Thy kingdom come, Thy will be done in earth, as it is in heaven.
Give us this day our daily bread.
And forgive us our debts, as we forgive our debtors.
And lead us not into temptation, but deliver us from evil: For thine
is the kingdom, and the power, and the glory, for ever. Amen.

—MATTHEW 6:9-13 KJV

DAY 42

The Poor

Give justice to the weak and the fatherless; maintain the right of the afflicted and the destitute. —**PSALM 82:3**

SOCIAL JUSTICE is the ability to love and maintain the rights, dignity, and worth of the afflicted and destitute. God loves the poor, and makes a special point within Scripture of defending them, and of expressing that we should love them, too. This is your daily reminder that social justice work refuses to engage in vilifying the poor, scapegoating the afflicted, and mistreating the destitute. The pursuit of social justice is a source of light in the dark, a form of hope for those desperately needing it.

The poor and destitute experience injustice more than most, because they often lack the resources to fight oppression. Unlike others, the poor literally can't afford to face injustice. Not all forms of injustice are affected by money, but the wealthy can use their finances to hire a lawyer, pay for security, lobby for political help, and acquire certain things to aid themselves. The poor are unable to afford the necessary tools required to defend themselves. Because of their financial vulnerability, they're especially exploited, taken advantage of, and helplessly left on their own—few willing to sacrifice their own wealth in order to help.

The poor are chastised and blamed for being too dirty, too lazy, too addicted to drugs and substances, too mentally unstable, too criminal, too unreliable, and too *inconvenient*. Few social institutions value them, and many prefer to discard them to the margins rather than commit any substantial time, effort, or finances towards helping them. To make matters worse, being poor is a hierarchical construct based on monetary worth—not divine love. Within societies that put a special emphasis on wealth and esteeming the rich, the poor are especially belittled. They're treated as social pariahs, faulted for failing to achieve what many consider life's ultimate purpose: to be rich.

The Bible says that "the love of money is a root of all kinds of evils. It is through this craving that some have wandered away from the faith and pierced themselves with many pangs" (1 Timothy 6:10). The poor are merely people who lack money. That's it. But who are they really? They're way more than we will ever know or realize. God understands this, and despite verse after verse proclaiming the importance of the poor, we can continue to miss out on appreciating their divine worth and value, even within our own lives. How foolish of us to judge someone by their monetary income. The truth is that some of the very poorest individuals on earth will also be the very richest ones within the kingdom of God.

Like Jesus, social justice work loves the poor. Social justice is dedicated to the lifelong practice of loving them, centering them, always keeping them in focus, never dehumanizing them, and never making them an afterthought of society. We should avoid the temptation to spiritually judge people based on their commercial input, economic status, or financial worth.

What Christian practice is best suited for stopping the oppression of the poor, for being generous to the needy, for honoring them, for knowing—and defending—the rights of the poor? The work of social justice.

MEDITATION

Whoever oppresses the poor shows contempt for their Maker, but whoever is kind to the needy honors God. —**PROVERBS 14:31 NIV**

The righteous care about justice for the poor, but the wicked have no such concern. —**PROVERBS 29:7 NIV**

"Because the poor are plundered, because the needy groan, I will now arise," says the Lord; "I will place him in the safety for which he longs." —**PSALM 12:5**

Whoever mocks the poor shows contempt for their Maker; whoever gloats over disaster will not go unpunished.
—PROVERBS 17:5 NIV

Do we avoid the poor in our lives? How can the poor become a centerpiece in our Christian existence?

Whoever is kind to the poor lends to the Lord, and he will reward them for what they have done. —**PROVERBS 19:17 NIV**

If anyone has material possessions and sees a brother or sister in need but has no pity on them, how can the love of God be in that person? —**1 JOHN 3:17 NIV**

When the poor and needy seek water, and there is none, and their tongue is parched with thirst, I the LORD will answer them; I the God of Israel will not forsake them. **—ISAIAH 41:17**

PRAYER

Dear God, help me to follow your example by prioritizing the poor. May I generously love them. Forgive me for the times I self-righteously judge them. I ask that my motivation for love not be pity or any perfunctory religious burden, but because the poor are deserving of my love. I want to see the poor as beloved individuals created in your divine image. Just as you accept me, let me accept them fully into my community, providing a place of belonging.

DAY 43

Love Is Power

When the righteous increase, the people rejoice, but when the
wicked rule, the people groan. —**PROVERBS 29:2**

A PARADOX of social justice work is that it gains more power by
giving it away. The more sacrificial the love for one's neighbor is, the
more effective it becomes. Social justice work sacrificially gives away
food, housing, healthcare, safety, jobs, education, transportation, and
money for the benefit of others. But the more valuable something is,
the harder it is to part with. Just as it's difficult to let go of our income
and wealth, it's similarly hard for people to share certain types of power.

What is power? Is it money, political influence, control? Or is
it love, justice, and mercy? There are different opinions about what
power is and isn't, but social justice work is founded on the principle
that everyone is powerful because every person in the world is made in
God's divine image, bestowed with a soul, presented with God-given
love, strength, dignity, and unsurpassable worth—power. When we
share our soul, and share our love, strength, dignity, and worth, and
allow others to realize that they are loved so that they can accept *their*
strength, dignity, and worth, we're doing social justice work.

Social justice work holds the very highest view of humanity. This is what inspires people to do social justice: a love of others. Dignity and worth are inherent in everyone, and they cannot be earned or achieved, and although they can be attacked, they cannot be taken away. Your neighbor is a human being of unlimited worth. So are you.

Superficial power assumes one's worth is associated with things, money, social status, influence, control, or other carnal attributes, where the emphasis is put on obtaining as much of it as possible because it is a limited resource. We will often try to hold on to these forms of power no matter the moral, spiritual, or human costs.

The pursuit of social justice helps us realize that divine power—the power in each and every human—is far more valuable than the superficial powers of mere things and stuff, the fleeting junk of this temporal existence. We must comprehend that the CEO holds just as much worth and dignity as the homeless person sleeping under the highway bridge, and that the president of the United States is just as valuable as the refugee applying for asylum. Social justice work has to be this way, because to manifest equity and justice, it must be fair and just. So, if the CEO experiences racism, social justice work takes up their cause just as passionately as it does trying to obtain affordable housing for the homeless person. The divine power of people should be treasured by us because it is revered by God. This is why God says that acts of social justice—helping others, protecting others, fighting oppression, and bringing justice, the manifestations of loving others—are priceless, while gold, wealth, and superficial power are worthless and will be destroyed by moth and rust.

When Jesus says, "For where your treasure is, there will your heart be also," he's telling us that our hearts should be with our neighbors (Luke 12:34). This sentiment is further reinforced by Jesus when he declares, "For whoever wants to save their life will lose it, but whoever loses their life for me and for the gospel will save it. What good is it for someone to gain the whole world, yet forfeit their soul?" (Mark

8:35-36 NIV). What does it profit a person if we gain the whole stock market, but lose our soul? Or gain fame and fortune, but lose our soul? Or achieve a successful professional career, but lose our soul? Or win an election, but lose our soul?

Social justice work is comfortable with losing, but not losing souls. Souls—humans—are our neighbors, living pieces of divine art, actual images of God, created by God, loved by God. Social justice work is comfortable losing money, friends, influence, and other things because it's the nature of sacrificial love. We must lose superficial power, privilege, fame, relationships, reputations, careers, money, and comfortability for the sake of love, mercy, and justice. Social justice work doesn't fret over loss because it comprehends that by losing it actually gains, because trading superficial power for the real power of relational love is a successful transaction.

As Christians who pursue social justice work, we can get great joy and hope from the reality of God's kingdom. God wants us to know that it's actually authentic. In the Bible, God uses the kingdom of God as motivation to follow and obey God's greatest commands. While most of the world—even many Christians—chase wealth and superficial power on earth, we can be people who attempt to follow God because we are citizens of God's kingdom. We're putting our hope in the belief that God's words are true, especially when God says that the most important thing is to love our neighbors. Social justice work loves, values, respects, and honors people. Because of this, whenever we participate in the work of social justice we love, value, respect, and honor God. Social justice work is an act of worship, a way to glorify God.

MEDITATION

The kingdom of heaven is like a grain of mustard seed that a man took and sowed in his field. It is the smallest of all seeds, but when it has grown it is larger than all the garden plants and becomes a tree, so that the birds of the air come and make nests in its branches. —**MATTHEW 13:31-32**

The kingdom of heaven is like treasure hidden in a field, which a man found and covered up. Then in his joy he goes and sells all that he has and buys that field. —**MATTHEW 13:44**

The kingdom of heaven is like a merchant in search of fine pearls, who, on finding one pearl of great value, went and sold all that he had and bought it. —**MATTHEW 13:45-46**

Do you believe in the power of love? How have you seen the love of God either be successful or unsuccessful within your own life? How can we prioritize loving people more than loving money or power?

As for the rich in this present age, charge them not to be haughty, nor to set their hopes on the uncertainty of riches, but on God, who richly provides us with everything to enjoy. They are to do good, to be rich in good works, to be generous and ready to share, thus storing up treasure for themselves as a good foundation for the future, so that they may take hold of that which is truly life. —**1 TIMOTHY 6:17-19**

PRAYER

God, help me to treasure people above all other things, above money, fame, power, comfort, security, entertainment, and acceptance. May I spend my life helping people recognize their divine worth, dignity, and power, and forgive me for the times I've mistreated others. Thank you for inviting me to be a part of your kingdom. I have yet to fully understand the reality of your kingdom, and the blessing that it is, but I'm grateful for it. You love me, and I love you.

Social Justice Begins With Us

And why worry about a speck in your friend's eye when you have a log in your own? How can you think of saying to your friend, "Let me help you get rid of that speck in your eye," when you can't see past the log in your own eye? Hypocrite! First get rid of the log in your own eye; then you will see well enough to deal with the speck in your friend's eye. —**MATTHEW 7:3-5 NLT**

THE WORK OF social justice starts within ourselves, and then flows out from within us into the lives of our surrounding families, friends, and communities. We can sometimes fool ourselves into thinking we're doing social justice work when we're actually just distracting ourselves with distant problems. It's not that the injustices occurring elsewhere are unworthy of our time or energy, because they are worthy. But we can make the mistake of using distant injustices as a convenient escape from the local injustices that demand our personal attention. Injustice is always much closer to home than we think.

Someone else's problems provide a good cover story for failing to take responsibility for our own problems. It's much easier to be doing social justice work elsewhere, where it doesn't require as much relational, emotional, or tangible investment. It's very difficult to face the injustices that are right in front of us, that involve the people closest to us, that impact our home, church, family, school, work, and neighborhood. It's easier to publicly chastise a stranger who committed abuse than it is to confront a sibling's abusive behavior. We're more comfortable spewing righteous anger against the sins of a foreign country than admitting our own nation's evils. Overall, it's always easier to uphold the standards of social justice work to our enemies, political opponents, and faceless outsiders than it is to uphold them to ourselves, or to those we know and love.

We all have people we need to confront, invest in, educate, apologize to, or make reparations to. Do we need to talk to our parents about their racist behavior, or have a discussion with our sibling about the xenophobic way they talk, or educate our friends about the importance of equity at school? We have countless opportunities to promote social justice within the social circles we live in, but sometimes it's easier to march against hateful strangers than have an honest conversation with someone we love. God has given us the strength to be bold enough to embrace these opportunities, because justice is worth it.

MEDITATION

Rather, speaking the truth in love, we are to grow up in every way into him who is the head, into Christ. —**EPHESIANS 4:15**

How do the people around you, whom you regularly interact with in your life, respond to your pursuit of social justice? Who do you know that needs to be confronted about their words, beliefs, or actions that contribute to injustice and oppression? What is a strategy for confronting them or working with them?

PRAYER

Dear God, show me the areas I need to grow in. Make me a truthful witness to your love of justice. Give me the humility to see my faults and ignorance. May I learn from those you send to teach me. Form me into a person who resists oppressors and finds solidarity with the oppressed. Give me the patience and strength to persist through humiliation, mistakes, conflict, and my own failures. Bestow upon me the wisdom and humility to know the difference between right and wrong, and the boldness to work to make myself a better representative of Jesus.

Social Justice Is Relational

We love because he first loved us. Whoever claims to love God yet hates a brother or sister is a liar. For whoever does not love their brother and sister, whom they have seen, cannot love God, whom they have not seen. And he has given us this command: Anyone who loves God must also love their brother and sister.

—1 JOHN 4:19-21 NIV

SOCIAL JUSTICE IS:

Visiting the elderly. Volunteering at a local elementary school. Buying groceries for the community food shelf. Coaching a kids' sports team. Teaching a class at a community center. Delivering meals. Working at a homeless shelter. Cleaning trash and litter at your local park. Rescuing an animal. Volunteering at a nursing home. Volunteering at a hospital. Leading a personal development class at a prison. Tutoring a child. Mentoring a teenager. Learning about a different culture. Fostering a child.

Social justice work is loving others. This love is manifested through action. Acts of service and actually *doing* good. Social justice work is participating in humanity and actively acknowledging the divine worth of those around us by relationally investing in them.

What happens when greed, corruption, or injustice prevents health-care to the elderly we visit, or defunds the local school we visit? Or shuts down the food shelf, or a child from the soccer team we coach is threatened with deportation? Or a student from our community center class learns that their family back in Syria died from a bomb, or that the meal pro-gram was cut from the city's budget, or someone from the homeless shel-ter was killed by gun violence? What happens when the park we frequent has been used to illegally dump industrial waste, or the animal rescue center was vandalized, or people at the nursing home are being abused? Or the patients we visit at the hospital can no longer afford treatment, or a prisoner in one of our classes has been assaulted by a guard, or a child we tutor has been evicted from their home? Or the teenager we're mento-ring is experiencing racism from a classmate, or we listen to a speaker talk about the difficulty of being a refugee in our community, or we learn from a foster child about the lack of educational resources they've had?

More often than not, social justice work is a gift given to us through our relationships with others. We often don't care about social justice work when we're disassociated from the greater relational world around us. When we isolate ourselves, restrict our relationships to an echo chamber of shared and singular worldviews, and become close-minded, we stop loving. Contrarily, we become the most passionate about social justice work when we're connected to a broader and more diverse com-munity, and it's our friends' lives, people we love, admire, and connect with, that serve as the inspiration for our acts of love.

There is a world around us waiting to be discovered, waiting to love and be loved, with people who will change our life in an unimag-inably wonderful way. How many neighborhoods are right next to us that we've never set foot in? How many people do we see every day that we never communicate with? Social justice work is connected to everyone, and the more relational we are, the more we'll understand the importance of our justice endeavors.

MEDITATION

Two are better than one,
   because they have a good return for their labor:
If either of them falls down,
   one can help the other up.
But pity anyone who falls
   and has no one to help them up.
Also, if two lie down together, they will keep warm.
   But how can one keep warm alone?
Though one may be overpowered
   two can defend themselves.
A cord of three strands is not quickly broken.

—ECCLESIASTES 4:9-12 NIV

How is social justice relational to you? Are you, or friends or family that you know, impacted by oppression and injustice? How have relationships hurt or helped your pursuit of justice?

PRAYER

Dear God, help me to lay down my life for my friends, and for my neighbors. I want to reflect your love to the community. May I be hospitable and kind to those you put in my path, and may my relationships with others be deep, meaningful, and full of goodness. Provide me with the bravery to risk starting new relationships, and to willingly press on when they fail. Help me not to give up on people, or even myself. Gift me the ability to laugh and cry with my neighbors, to truly know them, and may I be vulnerable and brave enough to allow them to know me, too. Thank you for the life you've given me, and may I bring love and justice to those around me.

Your Gifts

As each has received a gift, use it to serve one another, as good stewards of God's varied grace. —**1 PETER 4:10**

SOCIAL JUSTICE work, like Christianity, will eventually demand something of us. It's good to know about social justice, understand the causes of injustice, discover who the victims are, educate ourselves, and make ideological changes in order to accept the validity of pursuing justice. But knowing and doing are two different things, and social justice necessitates time, energy, and action. Without real-world applications that involve real decisions and real relationships, we can forget there are real movements that need real changes and practical outcomes. We should commit our most authentic self to accepting social justice work as being part of our real lives; otherwise justice, love, and mercy will die within the theoretical realms of superficial rhetoric.

You may feel underprepared, underqualified, or unworthy to participate, but those are the lies of resistance. Because God has created you for this exact moment in history, for the exact social justice movements that are happening right now. And you have more power and ability than you realize. As a Christian, you have the fruit of the Spirit: love, joy, peace, patience, kindness, gentleness, and self-control. With these holy weapons, any and all forms of social justice can be accomplished.

But you also have even more gifts. You have unique skills, professions, hobbies, networks, possessions, habits, and gifts that can be righteously used to love your neighbor. Do you know what they are? If not, ask your family and friends, because they definitely know what they are. Whether you believe it or not, you are vitally important to the movements that strive for love, mercy, and justice. You and your entire unique being are needed.

You are uniquely created by God to do social justice work. Social justice work needs cooks and bakers, writers and speakers, lawyers and clowns, babysitters and corporate executives, doctors and teachers, police officers and military veterans, artists and mathematicians, Christians and atheists, Democrats and Republicans, politicians and social workers, truck drivers and athletes, photographers and construction workers, professors and students, the young and the old. Social justice needs everyone involved because it impacts everyone. Are you organized? Good, help a food shelf run more efficiently. Are you a painter? Great, help repaint the rooms at the local homeless shelter. Are you a pastry chef? Wonderful, donate some lemon tarts to next month's anti-racism march. Do you work in human resources? Maybe you can initiate a project that would make your company's hiring practices more equitable. The opportunities are endless, and no skill or ability is too insignificant.

Christianity was never meant to be a religion that primarily manifested itself within a church building for a few hours each Sunday morning. No, it was originally a vast social movement led by Jesus, and it originated within the Roman Empire. What made it revolutionary was that it incorporated all sorts of people from all stations of society, and it united them towards a common goal: following Jesus. Similarly, this is what social justice is: a movement for justice, motivated and inspired by loving others. If this love and justice isn't manifested in people's lives, it doesn't exist. If social justice doesn't affect the way we work, learn, communicate, worship, travel, relate to others, facilitate government, and function as a society, it's pointless. Social justice work is not only a holy endeavor, but also a holistic endeavor, meant to right all social injustices throughout the world. Your gifts, skills, and abilities are required.

MEDITATION

Every good gift and every perfect gift is from above, coming down from the Father of lights, with whom there is no variation or shadow due to change. —**JAMES 1:17**

What unique gifts, skills, and abilities can you bring to a social justice movement?

PRAYER

Dear God, thank you for the gifts you have bestowed upon me. Help me to recognize them as holy and divine, worthy of being shared and appreciated. Give me the confidence to use them. May I not waste them, but help me steward my gifts in order to fight oppression and injustice. Thank you for the opportunity to serve my neighbors according to my unique abilities and capacities. Help me to celebrate and affirm the gifts of others. I pray that I'll encourage and inspire others to use their gifts in order to love, too. You are so generous and gracious to me. I love you.

DAY 47

Societal Theft

For I the LORD love justice; I hate robbery and wrong; I will faithfully
give them their recompense, and I will make an everlasting
covenant with them. —**ISAIAH 61:8**

GOD LOVES JUSTICE and hates robbery and wrongdoing. Our
society is filled with oppressive wrongdoing and various forms of theft,
and God's desire is for us to fix them. Social justice works towards
eliminating societal systems of theft. Social justice works on righting
the many things within our society that are wrong.

Education theft. Educational systems reflect the societal faults within
which they exist, so if structural racism, sexism, and other forms of
oppression are commonplace in political, economic, and religious systems, they'll equivalently exist in educational ones. This is why social
justice issues are interconnected with one another, influencing entire
ways of doing things, impacting and changing entire systems, redoing
the way a society functions.

Education systems can rob people of their potential and ability, miscategorizing a student's worth based on flawed testing techniques, mandated standards, inaccurate evaluation procedures, lack of funding, inequitable environments and accessibility, and systemic failures that are full of personal and corporate prejudices, discriminations, stereotypes, and biases. Education is full of interpersonal and systemic manifestations of oppression and injustice, and data has proved that these play a substantial role in a person's future outcomes. Variations in job placement rates, wage earning discrepancies, achievement gaps, criminal activity, the difference in graduation rates and college attendance, and many other indicators point to an entire system—like countless other societal structures—that are designed to benefit some and oppress others.

> My people will abide in a peaceful habitation, in secure dwellings, and in quiet resting places. —**ISAIAH 32:18**

Housing theft. All people deserve a home, a peaceful place to safely rest and live. So when refugees and immigrants are denied asylum and their attempt to find a new home is denied, it's a form of robbery. When rent gouging forces people to be evicted, and landlords are prejudiced against applicants, and affordable housing is sacrificed for the sake of corporate profits and property values, it's a form of robbery. When neighborhoods are redlined and closed off because of racism, it's a form of robbery. When loans are structured to fleece borrowers, and are denied to applicants because of discrimination, it's a form of robbery. As a society, we must stop robbing people and start giving them a place to live, a place to call home.

> Unequal weights are an abomination to the LORD, and false scales are not good. —**PROVERBS 20:23**

Voting theft. Many citizens cannot vote because of laws that prevent people convicted of crimes from voting. This is called disenfranchisement, and it prevents millions of Americans from exercising their right to participate in elections. Gerrymandering is another technique used to manipulate the way people can and can't vote, along with various voter suppression laws that make it harder for people to cast their vote—limiting the influence of people in order to benefit the power and privilege of a few. Whether it's through voting ID laws, voter purges, restricting voter registration, or propaganda campaigns aimed at undermining the outcome and legitimacy of elections, voting theft is an essential social justice issue. It's a matter of fair representation, and if millions of people are prevented from participating—or are unfairly disempowered—the system needs to be completely changed. When an electoral system is manipulated for the benefit of a few at the expense— and oppression—of the majority, it's tyranny.

> Behold, the wages of the laborers who mowed your fields, which you kept back by fraud, are crying out against you, and the cries of the harvesters have reached the ears of the Lord of hosts.
>
> **—JAMES 5:4**

Income theft. To deny someone their rightful due is theft. Perhaps no form of robbery has occurred on a grander scale than the modern era of reducing workers' salaries and wages. In a world where profits are an influential driving force for businesses, costs are often cut at the expense of employees. Benefits are lost, healthcare reduced or taken away, retirement investments cut, hours increased, employee protections removed, and wages reduced. Entire systems of work may get outsourced. In many situations, businesses use forced labor or labor with no legal oversight. While a company and its owners can reap record surpluses and appear healthy for investors, its workers may be suffering.

Today, the average salary for many people doesn't come close to accounting for cost-of-living increases and inflation. Many families have multiple people who hold multiple full-time jobs yet still struggle—through no fault of their own—to meet the basic costs of housing, healthcare, food, and education. Entire economic systems are structured to protect and value huge corporate interests rather than the welfare of humanity. Workers are being exploited.

Workers also face discrimination and salary inequities because of sexism, racism, ableism, ageism, and other forms of oppression. These are all forms of theft, depriving people of what they are rightfully owed. People also pay taxes, but do they get a proportional return on the amount they've given the government? Or do corporations end up getting billions in subsidies? Are military contractors receiving billions for new weapons? It's not just that people are being paid unfairly, it's that our society is devaluing the majority of people in order to appease the demands of the very rich, corporations, industrial behemoths, the war industry, and other special interest groups that use their wealth to lobby and influence governmental policies and decision-making at the expense of the well-being of humanity.

If a society cannot provide a livable wage to its population, and continually refuses to prioritize the majority of its population in order to bring continued wealth to a select few, the economic system needs to be restructured. Right now, the system benefits only a small minority while hurting the larger part of its citizenry. There's not a fair or equitable exchange of labor and compensation, wealth is hoarded, and the special interests of the rich and powerful are being prioritized—through lobbying, corruption, and political maneuvering—over the needs of the general population. Politicians, business leaders, and various oversight groups have failed to quell or reform abusive schemes of profiteering, so we must now act, because the current situation is unsustainable.

MEDITATION

Righteousness and justice are the foundation of your throne; steadfast love and faithfulness go before you. —**PSALM 89:14**

A false balance is an abomination to the LORD, but a just weight is his delight. —**PROVERBS 11:1**

Does everyone in your community have fair access to education, housing, voting, and income? What are some ways people are either intentionally or unintentionally excluded from these resources?

PRAYER

Dear God, I pray that my neighbors will always be provided with a fair education. I pray that they'll always have a place to call home. I pray that they'll be fairly represented with access to voting. I pray that they will have a livable income that enables them to thrive. If they don't have these things, may I be someone who helps provide these things. God, I want to thank you for providing for me in so many ways, and help me be wise enough to return the favor to my neighbors.

DAY 48

Slavery, Sexual Oppression, and Misogyny

Again I saw all the oppressions that are done under the sun. And behold, the tears of the oppressed, and they had no one to comfort them! On the side of their oppressors there was power, and there was no one to comfort them. —**ECCLESIASTES 4:1**

SLAVERY AND VARIOUS forms of sexual oppression have permeated societies for generations. The trauma and damage done by these evils are horrible, and social justice works to hold perpetrators accountable. It also celebrates the courage and witness of survivors. Slavery exists throughout the world and millions of people are entrapped in systems that commodify them. They're enslaved into forced labor. They're subjugated to sexual exploitation. Their identities are forcibly changed, and entire bodies are bought and sold and treated as property. The modern abolition movement is a social justice movement. It works to free people entrapped in slavery, imprisoned, and those who are trafficked and smuggled. Bodily theft also occurs through sexual abuse, sexual assault, and sexual harassment. Molestation, rape, sexual abuse, exploitation, and various other forms of sexual violence are major social justice issues.

Many people are also stuck in a penal system where they're forced into slave-like labor, given meager earnings, and in reality are stuck in a trap designed to produce cheap labor. Others are migrant workers, or refugees without a home, or children and teenagers. Due to poverty, war, violence, forced conscription, addiction, desperation, and deception, people are enslaved. Social justice is an abolition movement, a way to liberate people, to free them, to give hope and joy and justice.

As Christians, we must repent of our complicity in building systems that are misogynistic and predatory. We have preached destructive forms of patriarchy. We have objectified and dehumanized women and children under the guise of religious doctrine. Fear-driven forms of purity culture use shame and guilt to vilify, and our religion's failure to protect others, especially women, children, and LGBTQIA+ individuals, from sexual violence, abuse, harassment, and oppression has caused immense damage. The physical, emotional, and mental trauma caused by Christianity's crimes are expansive, and we must work to prevent these crimes from repeating and hold the criminals responsible. To do this we must open ourselves up to outside help and accountability, because we've proven that we often cannot effectively police ourselves.

The #MeToo movement exposed that our society, along with Christian institutions, have a long way to go until we end the widespread injustices of sexual violence, abuse, and harassment. We must work towards creating communities that are safe, open to accountability, and willing to believe survivors. We must learn and educate others about sexual violence and consent, and then make sure our systems and institutions have safeguards in place to protect people from harm. As Christians, we must never idolize money, power, fame, or our own reputations at the expense of our willingness or ability to look after the security and sexual well-being of others. Rather than embracing denial, Christians must accept reform, hold perpetrators accountable, make reparations, and work towards spreading a positive sexual ethic rather than an oppressive one.

Throughout history, women have been oppressed in many ways: denied their right to vote, limited in their professional vocations, constrained in their social freedoms, and dismissed in their emotional, physical, intellectual, and spiritual worth and abilities.

The hypocrisy and complicity of historic and continuing Christian oppression of women must also be fully acknowledged and confronted. It has allowed men to commit injustices while simultaneously vilifying feminism and promoting a "purity culture" built around shame, silence, and commodification of women. It has exalted male predators in leadership positions while weaponizing theology that prevented women from preaching, teaching, and using their God-given gifts. It has protected oppressors and assaulted victims.

Whether at church, work, school, or in homes, rampant harassment, abuse, rape, and other types of assault and violence plague women's lives. Their oppression has even been laughed at and doubted by people who continue to believe that women aren't equal. In fact, many still accept politicians who have allegedly assaulted women and publicly objectify them. Sexism is even celebrated as a partisan mark of allegiance, a brand of chauvinism that denigrates and dehumanizes. These physical oppressions reflect societal injustices that include earnings gaps and employment discrimination, education inequities, health care discrimination, and even biases within justice and legal systems. Social justice work calls upon us to help end all societal injustices against women.

MEDITATION

What are some practical ways you can help those suffering from slavery and sexual oppression within your own community? How can your religious community better confront sexual oppression? How can we hold our Christian communities accountable for sexual oppression?

For you have been a stronghold to the poor, a stronghold to the needy in his distress, a shelter from the storm and a shade from the heat; for the breath of the ruthless is like a storm against a wall. —**ISAIAH 25:4**

PRAYER

Dear God, I pray for those suffering from slavery, sexual oppression, or misogyny. Bring hope and healing. May you free them and provide justice. May they realize that it's not their fault. The society I live in can be a storm, a merciless place of cruelty, injustice, and oppression, but thank you for being a source of hope and strength, God. Help me to eradicate systems that are complicit in slavery, sexual oppression, and misogyny. Just as you advocate for the oppressed, may I advocate for them as well. I pray that survivors will be believed, and may I believe them, when they speak of their oppression. God, may I never judge them. May I pursue justice for them. May I bring comfort to them. Hold the oppressors accountable. Uplift survivors, and may their lives be blessed. I pray that they will be celebrated rather than shamed, and loved rather than ostracized. Thank you for being a God of justice.

DAY 49

⟵

Police Brutality

Then Pilate took Jesus and flogged him. And the soldiers twisted together a crown of thorns and put it on his head and arrayed him in a purple robe. They came up to him, saying, "Hail, King of the Jews!" and struck him with their hands. —JOHN 19:1-3

JESUS WAS APPREHENDED and physically abused by the authorities of his day. That the son of God experienced this type of injustice challenges our hearts to see Jesus as someone who can empathize with all those who are oppressed by people in positions of power.

Police brutality is a modern evil inherited and adapted from the historical atrocities of slavery and lynching. It is fueled by White supremacy and the societal systems that protect racism. Under the flimsy guise of "law and order" and "policing," violence and death are ruthlessly inflicted. No rationalization can excuse it. When police brutality is dispensed against people of color, it's not the victim's fault, or random bad luck, and it's not about being in the wrong place at the wrong time. No, it is law enforcement committing acts of wickedness.

It is centuries of systemic racism funneled into an overt attack against people of color. People are beaten, abused, unlawfully arrested, and murdered by police. And unless there's a perfect case that consists of video footage, witness testimonies, and a pile of evidence that can't be hidden or destroyed, police brutality usually occurs unopposed. The entire law enforcement system needs to change.

Let's come together and center the BIPOC (Black, Indigenous, and people of color) and queer voices who have long led the effort towards this abolition movement. We have the opportunity to acknowledge their truthful witness and accept their leadership. They have guided us to a place where we can admit that police systems were intentionally built to oppress others. As we work towards the liberation of those struggling against the weapons of policing, let's seek accountability, and bring justice to our schools, communities, homes, and churches.

Social justice work moves to rethink and restructure the entire system of policing in order to be more just and loving. For the sake of protecting our friends, family, and neighbors, we want policing that isn't violent, cruel, or oppressive. For the love of others we must do what's best, and to completely do something new is the most loving thing, because we cannot keep letting this injustice happen. To silently sit by as police brutality continues to wreak havoc on entire populations is to complicitly accept it as being an acceptable norm of society—it's not.

The burden is on us. Today we have the opportunity to be anti-racist and put in the work to stop police brutality. Today we have the opportunity to apologize for the generational terror we've let unfold, and for our active and passive involvement in it. Today we have the chance to atone for our silence, and for refusing to believe—or ignoring—the countless victims of police abuse. Publicly oppose racism. Denounce White supremacy. Together, let's do everything in our power to destroy it. Let's stand in solidarity with our BIPOC family, friends, and neighbors. March. Protest. Resist oppression. Lament with victims. Mourn with those who mourn. Diligently organize in order to make policy changes. Give reparations. Be an advocate, activist, and Christlike light that helps bring peace, justice, and love. We can do this.

MEDITATION

Greater love has no one than this: to lay down one's life for one's friends. —**JOHN 15:13 NIV**

Are you willing to lay down your life for our friends and neighbors being oppressed by police? What are some societal systems that claim to be good but are actually bad?

When the righteous cry for help, the LORD hears and delivers them out of all their troubles. The LORD is near to the brokenhearted and saves the crushed in spirit. —**PSALM 34:17-18**

PRAYER

Dear Jesus, the victim of brutality, help me to never forget that you were beaten and battered and incarcerated. Yet you are God. You see the injustice of police brutality as an abomination, and I pray that it will cease. I ask for the strength of the Holy Spirit to overcome the failed systems of policing and to build something better, something good and humane. Clear my heart and mind so that I never mistake legality as being the same thing as morality, or mistake cruelty as justice. May I never rejoice in the suffering of others, or be complicit in their injustice. Prince of Peace, give me the divine strength to be peaceful, and give me the determination and power to build a better way forward. Help me!

DAY 50

Prison Reform

To crush underfoot all the prisoners of the earth, to deny a man
justice in the presence of the Most High, to subvert a man in his
lawsuit, the Lord does not approve. —**LAMENTATIONS 3:34-36**

JESUS WAS ARRESTED and then put in jail. Other biblical personalities, including Joseph, Jeremiah, Micaiah, Daniel, Peter, John the
Baptist, Paul, James, and John, were all put in prison, too, arrested and
declared guilty by society.

Words and their associated meanings matter. Words like *prisoner*
and *incarcerated* might be associated with being guilty and being a
criminal, and for people living within the time of Jesus, these terms
applied to Christ and many of his followers. But these words and their
associative labels, though legally correct, weren't accurate descriptions
of their character, actions, or morals. Today, the incarcerated are often
described as "monsters," "parasites," and "animals," and because of this
they're often treated as such. These degrading terms, commonly used
by citizens, politicians, and various media, are attempts at denying

prisoners' divine worth, a worth that has been rightfully bestowed upon them by God.

In the same way, when we use the word *justice* within the context of *social justice*, we often use it in a sense that associates something being given to those who don't have it but deserve it: money for the poor, homes for the homeless, healthcare for the sick, freedom for the enslaved, justice for those who need it.

But when the word *justice* is used within the term *justice system*, pertaining to our society's laws, law enforcement, judiciary, and penal system, it's often thought of as a form of vengeance, retribution, or punitive act of judgment. Its associations go beyond what a person deserves, and instead become connected with our most depraved tendencies, lusting for a painful and vindictive edict. We may want "justice" to be served, or cheer when our favorite superheroes end up "getting justice" by destroying the villains in movies.

The state of prisons in the United States, and in many other nation-states, is not justice at all, but rather a merciless form of cruelty. The incarceration system, instead of creating justice, has perpetuated more injustice. For example, a person may have been arrested for having a small amount of drugs in their possession. If they are sentenced in court and put in jail, many would say that "justice was served." But what if this person, this person loved by God, was caged in a cell that lacked running water or contained open sewage, or left incarcerated for decades without the ability to leave, or placed in solitary confinement until they had a mental breakdown? What if this person was raped and assaulted in jail, or paroled only to be denied a job, a future career, or the ability to provide for their children? Is this "justice?" This is the reality for many millions of incarcerated people in the United States and around the world.

An honest examination of society's "justice systems" will show radical and unequal disparities, injustice on a massive scale. These disparities are often based on race, income level, partisan policies, and other socioeconomic factors. Justice systems are often *intentionally* structured to be racist, inequitable, and even managed with the intent of gaining enormous profits. Sentences can be absurdly long, cruel, or the result of incompetent, corrupt, or biased cops, witnesses, jurors, lawyers, judges, and laws. For too long the incarcerated have been used and abused by many different oppressors. Politicians incarcerate for partisan leverage to gain votes, and businesses lobby to incarcerate in order to gain a fortune off the misery and confinement of others. Police departments incarcerate to fill quotas, law enforcement officers incarcerate because of their personal biases and racist attitudes, and entire segments of society promote and accept imprisonment because of a misguided belief in punishment as justice. Penal systems have become modern forms of enslavement, where the scale of societal inequity and injustice can be fully witnessed.

People loved by God and created in God's image are being dehumanized through incarceration. This is a social justice matter of utmost importance. Rather than receiving justice, many incarcerated people are physically, mentally, and emotionally abused, deprived of basic human rights, and forced to suffer torturous conditions. Rather than receive help or support, inmates are often packed into overcrowded cells, denied civil and legal rights (often even stripped of their right to vote), coerced to do slave-like labor, and given cruel and sadistic punishments that ruin their lives instead of redeem them. These destructive environs break the human soul, and are anti-Christian in their design and functioning. To make matters worse, many prisons are privatized, so that the ultimate goal is to greedily make a profit rather than tending to a human in need. Instead of caring for the human soul, prisons have become a predatory system built into a billion-dollar industry.

When we dehumanize others, it's easier to accept their injustices as deserved and right, rather than fighting for justice on their behalf.

But Jesus calls us to pursue social justice for all people, in all places, for all time.

All of this isn't to say that people who commit crimes don't deserve to face consequences, or that they should be given a free pass. Rather, it's the desire that both the victim and the oppressor actually experience *justice*, and love, and mercy, rather than forms of torture, dehumanization, cruelty, trauma, abuse, racism, and *injustice*. Right now, our prison systems are unjust, broken beyond repair, and must be completely reworked.

> The Spirit of the Lord God is upon me, because the Lord has anointed me to bring good news to the poor; he has sent me to bind up the brokenhearted, to proclaim liberty to the captives, and the opening of the prison to those who are bound.
> —ISAIAH 61:1

Social justice work is the act of liberating people from oppression. To free captives and open prisons is a holy endeavor that will save people who are currently suffering under penal systems constructed to destroy them. Humane societies treat their incarcerated with dignity and care, ensuring justice through fairness and wisdom, not cruelty and brutality. Let's dedicate ourselves to helping the imprisoned, to show them mercy and love, to bring them justice.

MEDITATION

> So the band of soldiers and their captain and the officers of the Jews arrested Jesus and bound him. —JOHN 18:12

> Remember those who are in prison, as though in prison with them, and those who are mistreated, since you also are in the body. —HEBREWS 13:3

"For I was hungry and you gave me food, I was thirsty and you gave me drink, I was a stranger and you welcomed me, I was naked and you clothed me, I was sick and you visited me, I was in prison and you came to me." Then the righteous will answer him, saying, "Lord, when did we see you hungry and feed you, or thirsty and give you drink? And when did we see you a stranger and welcome you, or naked and clothe you? And when did we see you sick or in prison and visit you?" —**MATTHEW 25:35-40**

Do you consider Jesus to be a prisoner? Does your perception of people's worth and dignity change because they're in jail or labeled as a criminal? Have you ever been in prison or visited someone there? How much do you know about our prison system?

PRAYER

Dear Jesus the prisoner, help me to remember that you were a prisoner, incarcerated and declared guilty. Remind me that earthly justice systems are not only imperfect, but can be extremely unjust. I ask for the strength to pursue social justice on behalf of the incarcerated. I want eyes that see people as you see them, as divinely loved and made in your image. I want a heart that is like yours, full of compassion, kindness, and truth. May I bring justice just as you bring justice: through grace, mercy, fairness, and love.

DAY 51

Justice Systems

You shall do no injustice in court. You shall not be partial to the
poor or defer to the great, but in righteousness shall you judge your
neighbor. —**LEVITICUS 19:15**

ONE OF THE cruelest ironies of social justice work is that the very
justice systems of governments can be notoriously unjust. The legislative process, laws, law enforcement agencies, legal proceedings, judicial processes, prosecution, defense, and correctional systems are often
discriminatory and racist. As Christians, we should never glorify our
country's law enforcement, courts, or correctional systems at the cost
of denying the reality of oppression and injustice.

We cannot mistake social justice as being the same thing as legal
justice. The two are vastly different, and legality doesn't automatically
equate to morality. Many of the worst and most prominent human injustices were—and *are*—created, mandated, overseen, and propagated by
a country's judicial, legislative, and executive branches of government.
Slavery, segregation, and internment camps were all once perfectly legal

and socially acceptable. Evil still exists today, and it remains protected through the structures and systems of "law and order."

The pursuit of social justice recognizes that true crimes against humanity often go unpunished, and that justice goes beyond whether someone is found guilty or innocent in a court of law. Historically, participating in social justice has even been deemed illegal, and social justice continues to be criminalized today. Participating in social justice work will often be against the law. Just as injustice can be perfectly legal through unjust legislation and broken justice systems, social justice activists can be prosecuted under these same defective legal structures. The entire legal and justice system of our society is disproportionately oppressive to people of color, the poor, and various other groups of people.

Because of this merciless criminal justice system, people are robbed of their money, dignity, and life. Experiencing an unjustified encounter with the law is traumatic, often dehumanizing, and too often results in murder. This evil miscarriage of justice, where an entire system has been built to work for the benefit of the privileged few while simultaneously afflicting others, is an abomination to God, who embodies true justice. The life of Jesus centered around bringing justice to those who were maligned within their society. The gospel message is an account of how Jesus helps the poor, feeds the hungry, accepts the excluded, liberates the oppressed, and confronts the oppressors.

All our rhetoric about "liberty and justice for all," "innocent until proven guilty," and everyone's "right to counsel" means little when faced with the blatant injustices of a system intent on oppressing others. We must start working towards changing our society from a place of pseudo-martial law enforcement to one where people are treated humanely. This means transforming justice systems so that they'll use appropriate methods that value human dignity, recognize people's worth, and seek true justice. It's not unreasonable for everyone within a justice system, criminal and innocent alike, to receive equity, respect, mercy, and love.

Justice systems have been used to dehumanize and enslave, and they have been co-conspirators in many forms of oppression. Justice systems reflect a nation's heart and soul, revealing a society's worst sins or best virtues. If you want to know the state of a nation regarding racism, equity, and social justice, simply look at their justice system.

MEDITATION

Woe to those who decree iniquitous decrees, and the writers who keep writing oppression, to turn aside the needy from justice and to rob the poor of my people of their right, that widows may be their spoil, and that they may make the fatherless their prey! What will you do on the day of punishment, in the ruin that will come from afar? To whom will you flee for help, and where will you leave your wealth? —**ISAIAH 10:1-3**

Do you think your local and national justice system is fair and just? Why or why not?

PRAYER

Dear Jesus the criminal, your status as a criminal reminds me of how easily justice systems can get things so completely wrong. May I never become apathetic towards those unfairly treated, and help me to speak up for the innocent who are falsely labeled as criminals. Inspire me to work towards breaking down unjust systems so I can help the oppressed. Thank you for being the perfect judge, and thank you for also taking the form of a criminal, showing me the futility of social status and labels, and teaching me that everyone—even criminals—is worthy of my love. Forgive me for my mistaken assumptions and bad judgments, and protect me from having a hard and cynical heart. You are my hope for a future kingdom with perfect justice, but for now I pray that you'll renew my strength as I engage in a broken world full of broken systems. I pray that you'll help me to love my neighbors who are suffering within broken justice systems.

Love Your Neighbor More Than Your Religion

Let all that you do be done in love. —**1 CORINTHIANS 16:14**

God desires that we always center our faith upon love. But it can be hard to keep our love free from religious qualifiers and technicalities. Love can be contradictory to the systems and environments we live within. We may constrain God's love through the legal framework of our government, by labeling people as illegal or legal, and by oppressing them through jail, deportation, or restricting their rights. God's love can be opposed through the theological positions of a church denomination, by excluding people from communion, marriage, or other practices. Societal biases can negate God's love by tempting us to dehumanize and vilify the same people society does. Through everything, God calls us to love.

Let all of our social justice work be done in love. May we not over-spiritualize everything, and never let our faith distract us from being a loving neighbor. Following Jesus inspires us to be a loving neighbor, and sometimes we need to reduce everything to its most basic principles. For Christians this means to love God and to love our neighbors.

> Love does no wrong to a neighbor; therefore love is the fulfilling of the law. —**ROMANS 13:10**

One of the greatest tragedies of many models of Christianity is that we teach proper doctrine instead of practicing neighborly love. Our churches, preachers, and theologians debate, argue, and fight about theological principles, biblical interpretations, and all sorts of things that really aren't that important. Meanwhile, the communities around us aren't being loved, and the oppression and injustice occurring right within our midst is left unaddressed. We don't need to be a theologian to love our neighbors. We don't need to hold a ministerial license or seminary degree to love our neighbors. What is required is our love.

God would rather we be a good neighbor than a good theologian, good preacher, or good biblical scholar. In fact, the best theology of all is this: to love God and love our neighbors. So let's not distract ourselves with the never-ending ways we can dive into religious fundamentalism and extremism. Instead, let's try being a better neighbor. To be a good Christian is to be a loving neighbor. Jesus is love. He's the manifestation of God and the very embodiment of God's love. We can learn how to love others by emulating the life of Jesus. This is what the gospel message invites us to do: to love others just as Jesus did.

MEDITATION

Is our faith fueled by love? What religious things prevent us from loving our neighbors?

> Little children, let us not love in word or talk but in deed and in truth. —**1 JOHN 3:18**

Beloved, let us love one another, for love is from God, and whoever loves has been born of God and knows God. —**1 JOHN 4:7**

PRAYER

Dear God, may I always follow you, especially if and when our religion diverges from your greatest commands. Help me to always love you and love my neighbors more than I love my preferred theological doctrines, religious traditions, and spiritual rhetoric. Your word tells me that love is everything, that it's the most important thing of all. So may I become more loving with each passing day. I praise you for exuding your perfect love through your words, actions, and deeds. Thank you so much for loving me, for loving everyone.

DAY 53

Healthcare

I was sick and you visited me. —**MATTHEW 25:36**

A PERSON DESERVES physical and mental healthcare because it's their human right. One's ability to receive first aid, tend to an injury, have medication, see a doctor, treat an illness, and get healthcare shouldn't be determined by the strength of one's insurance, income level, or perceived social status. Someone who needs physical or mental care should be able to receive it because they're a human being.

Unfortunately, various injustices prevent the proper facilitation of healthcare. The goal for many healthcare practices and systems isn't that patients are immediately given the best treatment, but that they're given the most profitable ones. The sick aren't healed completely, but only according to what their insurance or finances allow. Medical facilities are run as businesses, and those who can't afford to pay sometimes end up paying with their lives.

The desperate may resort to asking for donations or starting fundraisers with the hope of earning even a fraction of the costs necessary to get help. Others simply give up, resigned to the fact that they'll never be in the privileged position of receiving the best— or any—medical attention. Some would sacrifice their own health rather than send their family into poverty, or force their loved ones to take on an insurmountable amount of debt.

As Christians, we are called to care for the sick, and many do a good job of this. Paying off medical debt is a great way to combat inequitable healthcare practices. Providing free services is also a wonderful method for medical practitioners to selflessly love those within their communities. Many churches practice doing medical mission trips, where professionals are sent to other countries in order to help those in need, and a similar mindset needs to take root even within the most ostensibly wealthy of societies, where healthcare is inaccessible to many.

Social justice work protects life, and works to give people their best possible life, full of healing and health. Healthcare, medical treatment, and medicine are all vital social justice issues. If the care of a person's health becomes determined upon anything other than their humanity, society has become lost. So we must change the way people are prevented, blocked, and exploited by various oppressive and unjust medical systems and practices. Treatment must be fair, nondiscriminatory, affordable, and accessible. Remember the story of the good Samaritan? He was credited by God with caring for the man's injuries: "He went to him and bound up his wounds, pouring on oil and wine. Then he set him on his own animal and brought him to an inn and took care of him" (Luke 10:34). May we be good Samaritans within our communities.

MEDITATION

Do you think healthcare needs to be changed? Is it fair and just, or does it discriminate?

PRAYER

God, I pray that I will tenderly love those who need care. Help me to bring comfort to the sick, and healing to the body, spirit, mind, and soul of my neighbors. You have brought me so much healing, comfort, and peace. Give me a desire to use my life to bring such blessings to others. When I encounter someone in need I ask for an opportunistic spirit of thankfulness rather than sorrow, dread, or resignation. I want to value humanity in such a way that I want people to receive the very best medical attention. Enable me to protect and care for life instead of destroying or exploiting it. You love me in sickness or in health, and it's my prayer that I will love my neighbors in the same way.

DAY 54

Environmentalism

In the beginning, God created the heavens and the earth.
—GENESIS 1:1

THE FOUNDATIONAL principle of social justice work is to love God's creations, specifically people, but the same principle applies to loving God's non-human creations, too: land, waters, animals, plants, the air we breathe. The universe, and the planet we live on, is a creation of God, and if God creates anything, it's definitely worth caring for. To abuse the earth, or destroy parts of it, is literally abusing and destroying parts of God's own creation.

On the glorious splendor of your majesty, and on your wondrous works, I will meditate. **—PSALM 145:5**

The beauty of God is displayed through the glorious revelations of nature. The psalmist reflects the awe of God by saying, "When I look at the night sky and see the work of your fingers—the moon and the stars you set in place—what are mere mortals that you should think about them, human beings that you should care for them?" (Psalm 8:3-4 NLT). The apostle Paul wrote, "For his invisible attributes, namely, his eternal power and divine nature, have been clearly perceived, ever since the creation of the world, in the things that have been made" (Romans 1:20).

God's divinity is manifested by the grandeur of time, space, the endless matter around us, and the very world that God created. But when we pollute the air, poison the water, mismanage the land, greedily exploit natural resources, participate in animal cruelty, and practice or support policies that hurt the world, we destroy its beauty. May we not erase the beauty that God has created. When we harm our environment, we're withholding the unique glory of God that's witnessed through the awesome magnificence of a healthy, thriving, unpolluted world.

Caring for God's creation is a vitally important social justice issue because God's creation is a conduit for God's glory. God's glory is revealed in many ways, but nature is one powerful way many people connect to God. They see God's handiwork. They commune with God because they can feel God's presence. But what if there was no nature? What if the earth was spoiled beyond comprehension, with God's creation so destroyed that it actually pointed to no God existing at all? If instead of a pristine lake surrounded by healthy trees, what if there was a toxic landfill with so much pollution that the sun was constantly blotted out? What if the harmful effects of a befouled land caused cancer to residents who lived nearby, and then those victims suffered miserably from their sicknesses? Would God be glorified by these horrors? Of course not.

Caring for the environment also directly helps care for the people living within it. Oppression and injustice can be directly associated with our physical environment. Many major cities can trace the formation of their poorest and most impoverished communities back to industrial facilities and the pollution that came with them. Downwind. Downriver. In the midst of chemicals, sewage, industrial byproducts, and all sorts of contagions and contaminations. These were where the maligned of society were allotted to live, forced to suffer amid the worst environs. Even today, many of the world's poorest and most oppressed communities are trapped in squalor, often in areas unfit for human habitation, places ruined by war, industry, or other forms of social mismanagement. They often don't have access to healthy physical environments, where they can enjoy the world as it was meant to be: with clean air, clear water, unpolluted wilderness, unspoiled places free of noise pollution, smog, or harmful waste. The oppressed often exist within physical environments that are unnaturally corrupted, ruined, and experiencing a slow death, which in turn creates an unhealthy body, mind, and spirit.

How we interact with the natural and physical world around us reflects our interactions with God. Living things are God's creations. If you haven't already done so, develop a theology around how you treat the earth, animals, and all living things. Because God watches over them. So consider God when you see the splendor of the lilies of the fields and birds of the air, when you use the rocks and water and air, and remember that God watches. God *sees*.

Caring for the world, our planet, the environment, and all the living things around us is a Christian duty bestowed upon us by God. Our divine calling to wisely steward God's creation is a life and death responsibility, and we honor God by fulfilling our charge to protect the earth by blessing its people with a healthy environment.

MEDITATION

What role does environmentalism play within your spirituality? How does taking care of the planet, animals, and living things fit into the Christian faith?

PRAYER

Dear God, thank you for creation! May I find awe by reflecting upon your wondrous universe, and when I see the natural beauty of the world let it remind my heart of your greatness. Be glorified by your handiwork. Let the earth, stars, and space sing praises to you, and may they reveal to my soul the mysteries of your holy splendor! Forgive me for spoiling your work, for mistreating and exploiting what you have gifted to humanity. I pray that I'll appreciate the scope of your grand designs, and that I will recognize and pursue the purpose of my life within this vast and infinite existence. I want to be a worthy caretaker of your divine work, lovingly and thoughtfully fulfilling my duty to wisely respect the environment and all living things. God, help me be a good steward of your world.

DAY 55

Indigenous Land

Treasures gained by wickedness do not profit, but righteousness
delivers from death. —**PROVERBS 10:2**

WE SOMETIMES prefer ignorance over truth because it's easier to live without the weight of responsibility and the burden of pursuing justice. Ignorance invites us to be blissfully uninvolved, and requires no moral, practical, or relational demands of us. Maybe no clearer example of this exists than doing a historical investigation into who previously owned the land on which we now live, work, and profit. Because at one point in the past, maybe even relatively recently, the land was owned by someone other than us, our church, or our workplace, and chances are it was stolen, either through exploitation or violent force.

Find out who originally inhabited the land you're on. It's a simple exercise that will introduce you to hard truths, but truths nonetheless. In doing this, you'll learn about justice and injustice, and view history through the lens of others.

Identify the victims, and honor their suffering of injustice by being a truthful witness and sharing their histories. As a witness, identify the oppressors, and pursue justice by seeking fair and necessary judgments and reparations.

As followers of Jesus, we must accept historical truths instead of ignoring them. Actions have consequences, and the atrocities of the past still have present-day ramifications. Injustice doesn't just spontaneously happen, but is manifested over generations.

The oppressed are the first to understand this, because they're often the first victims to face the realities of horror. These people *know* the pain, even as entire societies ignore them. It's these people that Jesus intimately knows, whom he attempts to introduce his disciples and followers to. Most of the time, just like the initial reaction of his disciples, people don't understand. They criticize Jesus for meeting with children, Samaritans, women, prostitutes, tax collectors, and all the others deemed to be unclean and not good enough. But how does Jesus primarily manifest the gospel, the new truth that will save humanity? Christ goes out and commits social acts of justice and goodwill. His message of salvation and hope is a campaign of social justice.

Jesus feeds the hungry, heals the sick, empowers the powerless. And he does not present salvation as an academic list of theological principles, but instead commands that his followers do these same things—commit social acts of justice and goodwill. This is also our responsibility today, and we must reconcile the injustices of the past that still haven't been resolved.

Indigenous people are not just a past history lesson. They are a living people who are presently made in the image of God. We must honor their past by recognizing the injustices they experienced, and ally with them now as they continue to pursue justice and seek reparations. One practical way we can start this is to begin the habit of tracing land ownership. So today, learn who originally owned the land you're now on, and make it a lifelong discipline.

MEDITATION

Who once owned the land you live on, the land of your present-day community?

PRAYER

God, forgive me for my greed, my apathy, and my historical ignorance and revisionism. I pray that I will see the truth no matter how shameful or difficult it may be. Give me the wisdom and strength to apologize and make things right.

DAY 56

Apologize

*Therefore, confess your sins to one another and pray for one
another, that you may be healed.* —**JAMES 5:16**

ROMANS 3:23 declares that "all have sinned and fall short of the
glory of God," and yet taking responsibility for our sins and practicing
the important act of apologizing isn't always a common discipline within Christianity. For Protestants, part of the problem is the abandoned
practice of public confession. Often associated with the Catholic tradition, it's been phased out of many church routines.

There have also been historical and modern abuses of confession,
such as requiring the payment of unfair penances, or apologies resulting in public shame, humiliation, ostracization, and even excommunication. Obstructing public confession is also a tactic used by abusers
and predators as a way to quell their own guilt and to enable their
continued acts of oppression. Privacy and "forgiving each other" within the narrow confines of a closed and restrictive spiritual community
are among the greatest tools of perpetrators, and prevent victims from
receiving the justice they deserve.

But apologizing is an important part of social justice work—and one with great biblical precedent. Apologizing admits our role in perpetuating injustice. It honors the victims of oppression and works to establish justice for them. Apologizing should be proactive. It should never be a last resort or a forced act of public pressure. It's not meant to be a begrudging concession. Instead, it should be earnest and true. An apology should first and foremost prioritize the victim. An apology should primarily benefit the victim. It should always center the victim.

We should clearly and concisely admit our personal and corporate wrongdoings, and withhold rationalizations or excuses or anything else that attempts to disqualify our own responsibility. We must own it.

How will we make it right? Are reparations required? If so, clearly state how we will bring about justice. If we don't know how to do this, we must be prepared to ask the victims themselves how to make it right, and to listen to them and validate their responses. What action steps are being taken to right the wrongs, and what are we doing to guarantee these wrongs won't be committed again in the future? Apologies should include these things, and it's important that we start normalizing the Christian act of apologizing.

Christians shouldn't mistakenly believe that apologizing discredits everything good a person has ever said or done. Saying "I'm sorry" doesn't disqualify you from being a Christian or being a good person. In fact, genuine apologies reflect a Christlike humility. Apologizing promotes honesty, transparency, authenticity, and truth — things all Christians should exhibit throughout their lives. When Christians apologize, it adds integrity and legitimacy to our words and actions.

But apologizing also doesn't negate the consequences of our actions. A huge part of apologizing is accepting responsibility and committing to make it right. Legally, this may in some cases require financial compensation, time spent in jail, and inheriting a criminal record. It will also require discomfort, sacrifice, and a willingness to make amends—however costly they may be.

As Christians, we need to continuously work on apologizing, because we all have a lot to apologize for. When our pastors, leaders, churches, and organizations sin against our neighbors and communities, we must apologize. We've been silent for too long. Throughout the New Testament, Jesus is constantly correcting his disciples and holding them accountable—we need to do the same.

Apologizing is a sacred act. We must passionately pursue the role of being humble servants who fiercely love everyone, and apologizing is intrinsic to loving. Imagine how the world would be different if Christians throughout history had been brave enough to say these two simple words: "I'm sorry."

I'm sorry for the church's historical and present-day role within White supremacy. Our participation in slavery, segregation, and the physical, spiritual, and emotional violence inflicted upon Black people, Indigenous people, and all people of color is horrendously evil. The way we have upheld and promoted systemic racism for generations, and continue to do so, is not just wrong, but anti-Jesus.

I'm sorry for the church's historical and present-day role within child abuse: the sexual abuse and exploitation of children has destroyed countless lives, and has been covered up rather than apologized for.

I'm sorry for the church's historical and present-day misogyny: the denigration and abuse of women, denying them roles within ministry and leadership positions, and theologizing them as less-than, unworthy, and the cause of all sin and pain and suffering.

I'm sorry for the church's historical and present-day actions against LGBTQIA+ individuals: denying them their humanity, their right to marry and live and love, and working relentlessly to vilify them as inherently immoral.

I'm sorry for the church's historical and present-day hatred for immigrants and refugees: failing to provide a refuge and a safe shelter for those in need, and refusing to welcome our neighbors, or to recognize them as people loved by God. For our willingness to cage and incarcerate the most vulnerable, to deport them, to separate them from their families and loved ones.

I'm sorry for the church's historical and present-day role in oppressing foreigners: instigating countless wars and global interventions in order to steal wealth, power, and influence. I'm sorry for the unspeakable violence and suffering brought upon entire countries and people groups for the sake of political gain, misguided fear, racism, and the potent mix of nationalism, White supremacy, xenophobia, and capitalism.

I'm sorry for the church's historical and present-day role in oppressing non-Christians. I'm sorry for all the violence inflicted on others due to Christians' lust for power and wealth.

I'm sorry for the church's historical and present-day roles in all forms of corruption, violence, inequity, racism, hate, bigotry, ableism, ageism, greed, manipulation, deception, betrayal, abuse, oppression, theft, White supremacy, anti-Semitism, xenophobia, and all moral, emotional, intellectual, spiritual, political, economic, and societal failures.

Christianity has dehumanized and sinned against so many people, all of whom are divinely loved by God and uniquely made in God's image. Lament. Apologize. Make amends.

MEDITATION

Whom do you need to apologize to?

> Whoever conceals their sins does not prosper, but the one who confesses and renounces them finds mercy. —**PROVERBS 28:13 NIV**

PRAYER

Dear God, open my eyes to the wrongs I've committed against my neigh-
bors. Soften my heart and transform my mind. Help me to take respon-
sibility for my transgressions and give me the boldness and bravery to
apologize. I'm so grateful for your forgiveness towards me. Please remind
me of the endless grace, mercy, and love that you never withhold from me.
Your generosity knows no end, and you willingly sacrificed your life for
me. So I ask that I'll always make things right with those I've wronged.

Reparations

"Behold, Lord, the half of my goods I give to the poor. And if I have defrauded anyone of anything, I restore it fourfold." And Jesus said to him, "Today salvation has come to this house." —**LUKE 19:8-10**

IN THESE VERSES, Zacchaeus, who is a tax collector, makes a promise to Jesus that he will make reparations to those he may have defrauded, committing to give back fourfold. Jesus is *very* pleased by this.

Apologizing becomes null and void if there's no commitment to justice. A true apology goes beyond mere rhetoric, and actually works to make things right. This is the necessary role of making reparations, to make amends for the wrongs that have been done.

Consider this passage in Matthew:

Therefore, if you are offering your gift at the altar and there remember that your brother or sister has something against you, leave your gift there in front of the altar. First go and be reconciled to them; then come and offer your gift.

> Settle matters quickly with your adversary who is taking
> you to court. Do it while you are still together on the way, or your
> adversary may hand you over to the judge, and the judge may
> hand you over to the officer, and you may be thrown into pris-
> on. Truly I tell you, you will not get out until you have paid the last
> penny. **—MATTHEW 5:23-26 NIV**

The principle Jesus is trying to communicate is that you cannot be in a right relationship with God while simultaneously being in a wrong relationship—an unjust relationship—with your neighbor. Before you give to God, make sure you have made reparations to those who've been wronged.

One of the major themes of Christianity is that God gives people an abundance of grace, mercy, and love, way more than they actually deserve. At the very least, we should strive to emulate this godly atti-tude to those around us. But beyond that, reparations are deserved by the victims of injustice. Reparations aren't an act of charity or gift, they're a debt owed to our neighbor. God expects us to pay this debt back to them. Those who have been wronged deserve to receive amends—this is what love and justice is. If we cannot even pay back those who've been wronged by us, we aren't even meeting the bare minimum of God's expectations of us.

To pursue social justice requires making reparations. By with-holding reparations, we're engaging in the most diabolical form of hypocrisy, where we receive undeserved blessings from God while simultaneously denying our neighbors the restitutions they rightfully deserve from us.

Reparations constitute the final stage of admitting truth. First there's lament, then apologizing, but without the ultimate act of repa-ration, any lament or apology becomes invalidated. Without any real or quantifiable recompense—of land returned, income restored, wages increased, healthcare given, finances provided—our work just becomes a form of superficial religious pandering and empty activism.

MEDITATION

Who do you need to make reparations to? How will you do so?

> If anyone, then, knows the good they ought to do and doesn't do it, it is sin for them. —**JAMES 4:17 NIV**

PRAYER

God, what is more valuable than the people you love? What is worth more than the people you created in your divine image? May I make reparations for the wrongdoings that have been committed against my neighbors, and in doing so glorify and honor you.

DAY 58

Rest for the Weary

Come to me, all who labor and are heavy laden, and I will give you
rest. Take my yoke upon you, and learn from me, for I am gentle
and lowly in heart, and you will find rest for your souls.

—MATTHEW 11:28-29

JESUS RESTED, and so should you. Social justice is hard work.
It requires moments of pause, reflection, and deep rejuvenating rest.
Rest isn't escapism, it's the necessary action required to participate for
the long haul. Fighting oppression and injustice exposes us to horrific
things that can sap our physical, mental, and spiritual strength. Your
soul will need nourishment.

So regularly take time to check in on yourself and others. How is
your state of being? How is your overall health? Make sure you're doing
okay. Seek help if you need it. Go to therapy, confide in friends, take
some time off, set up boundaries. Make sure you're receiving support
from others, and don't try to go it alone. Social justice, like Christianity,
is a communal experience. Encourage each other.

Therefore encourage one another and build one another up, just as you are doing. —**1 THESSALONIANS 5:11**

One of the ways evil resists social justice is by bombarding people with a constant assault of bad news. Crime. Corruption. Violence. Death. All of the many manifestations of oppression and injustice will try to destroy our soul. The sheer magnitude of injustice and the seemingly impossible amount of work that needs to be accomplished in order to overcome it can overwhelm even the most seasoned social justice champion. So allow yourself time to rest, to receive help, to pause. Be graceful and merciful to yourself, and give yourself permission to recover and be comforted. The same abundance of love we show to others must also be given to ourselves.

MEDITATION

The LORD is my shepherd; I shall not want.
>He makes me lie down in green pastures.
He leads me beside still waters.
>He restores my soul.
He leads me in paths of righteousness
>for his name's sake.

Even though I walk through the valley of the shadow of death,
>I will fear no evil,
for you are with me;
>your rod and your staff,
>they comfort me.

You prepare a table before me
>in the presence of my enemies;

you anoint my head with oil;
  my cup overflows.

—PSALM 23:1-6

Do you rest enough? Have you ever reached a point of burnout? What does this look like? How can you encourage others and be a source of rejuvenation and comfort?

And he said to them, "Come away by yourselves to a desolate place and rest a while." For many were coming and going, and they had no leisure even to eat. **—MARK 6:31**

The LORD is near to the brokenhearted and saves the crushed in spirit. **—PSALM 34:18**

Fear not, for I am with you; be not dismayed, for I am your God; I will strengthen you, I will help you, I will uphold you with my righteous right hand. **—ISAIAH 41:10**

PRAYER

Dear God, thank you for being a divine source of peace, rest, and comfort. Take me within your arms and hold me. Allow me to believe in the reality of the love you have for me, and convince me of the truth that your love is endless and without qualifiers. Thank you for always loving me. You are my shield and fortress and salvation, an ever-present help. I abide in you, I rest in you. Renew my mind, body, and spirit. You are here with me, right now, in this very moment. Thank you for never leaving my side.

DAY 59

God of Justice

Then I saw a great white throne and him who was seated on it.
From his presence earth and sky fled away, and no place was found
for them. And I saw the dead, great and small, standing before the
throne, and books were opened. Then another book was opened,
which is the book of life. And the dead were judged by what was
written in the books, according to what they had done.
—REVELATION 20:11-12

THERE WILL BE a reckoning for the oppressor, and justice *will* be
served. *Nobody* can escape God's judgment. The judgment of God has
often been used as a form of spiritual manipulation and as a fearmon-
gering tool. It's used to scare people into following certain doctrines, or
as spiritual leverage, threatening eternal damnation on people if they
don't convert, join a particular church, or adhere to certain doctrines.

But in reality, God's judgment is the ultimate victory over oppression and injustice. It's a form of liberation. The wicked will be pun-
ished, and those who may have escaped justice or accountability on
earth will receive their due. God cannot be cheated. This is the ultimate

hope and truth of social justice: that God's love and justice prevails. The kingdom of God *will* be fully enacted, and oppression and injustice will cease to exist. Victims will rejoice. The oppressed will be free, their burdens gone, their lives restored, their spirits uplifted!

When Jesus is in the process of being tortured to death on the cross, he manages to mutter this infamous phrase: "My God, my God, why have you forsaken me?" This is the cry of all victims of oppression and injustice. "Why is this happening?! Why us?! Where is justice?! Where is our salvation?!" Far too often, the guilty go free, the oppressors face no consequences, or even are rewarded with wealth and power for their cruelty. It's not fair. Where is God in all of this?

The people watching Jesus as he's being murdered on the cross would have immediately recognized what Jesus was saying. It was a reference to Psalm 22. The first portion of the Psalm is a cry to God, asking why God would allow such injustice to occur in the world. It's the cry that all victims of injustice can relate to. "Why?!" Jesus musters just enough strength to utter these words, "Why have you forsaken me?!" But there's a poetic beauty happening here that often goes undetected by the modern reader. Because Jesus is directing people, the witnesses who are watching him die, to a psalm of justice.

Although Psalm 22 begins as a lament to God, it ends by reinforcing the magnificence of God's ultimate justice and love for the oppressed. The psalm ends with these prophetic and true words:

> I will tell of your name to my brothers;
>> in the midst of the congregation I will praise you:
> You who fear the LORD, praise him!
>> All you offspring of Jacob, glorify him,
>> and stand in awe of him, all you offspring of Israel!
> For he has not despised or abhorred
>> the affliction of the afflicted,

and he has not hidden his face from him,
  but has heard, when he cried to him.
From you comes my praise in the great congregation;
  my vows I will perform before those who fear him.
The afflicted shall eat and be satisfied;
  those who seek him shall praise the LORD!
May your hearts live forever!

—PSALM 22: 22-26

In the end, God saves the oppressed. He doesn't forsake or abandon the oppressed, but delivers them. God has heard the cries of those experiencing injustice, and "The afflicted shall eat and be satisfied." As Jesus is dying from injustice, he declares that God wins—justice and love win—in the end.

MEDITATION

My God, my God, why have you forsaken me?
  Why are you so far from saving me, from the words of my
    groaning?
O my God, I cry by day, but you do not answer,
  and by night, but I find no rest.

Yet you are holy,
  enthroned on the praises of Israel.
In you our fathers trusted;
  they trusted, and you delivered them.
To you they cried and were rescued;
  in you they trusted and were not put to shame.

But I am a worm and not a man,
  scorned by mankind and despised by the people.

All who see me mock me;
    they make mouths at me; they wag their heads;
"He trusts in the Lord; let him deliver him;
    let him rescue him, for he delights in him!"

Yet you are he who took me from the womb;
    you made me trust you at my mother's breasts.
On you was I cast from my birth,
    and from my mother's womb you have been my God.
Be not far from me,
    for trouble is near,
    and there is none to help.

Many bulls encompass me;
    strong bulls of Bashan surround me;
they open wide their mouths at me,
    like a ravening and roaring lion.

I am poured out like water,
    and all my bones are out of joint;
my heart is like wax;
    it is melted within my breast;
my strength is dried up like a potsherd,
    and my tongue sticks to my jaws;
    you lay me in the dust of death.

For dogs encompass me;
    a company of evildoers encircles me;
they have pierced my hands and feet
I can count all my bones—
they stare and gloat over me;
they divide my garments among them,
    and for my clothing they cast lots.

But you, O Lᴏʀᴅ, do not be far off!
>O you my help, come quickly to my aid!
Deliver my soul from the sword,
>my precious life from the power of the dog!
>Save me from the mouth of the lion!
You have rescued me from the horns of the wild oxen!

I will tell of your name to my brothers;
>in the midst of the congregation I will praise you:
You who fear the Lᴏʀᴅ, praise him!
>All you offspring of Jacob, glorify him,
>and stand in awe of him, all you offspring of Israel!
For he has not despised or abhorred
>the affliction of the afflicted,
and he has not hidden his face from him,
>but has heard, when he cried to him.

From you comes my praise in the great congregation;
>my vows I will perform before those who fear him.
The afflicted shall eat and be satisfied;
>those who seek him shall praise the Lᴏʀᴅ!
>May your hearts live forever!

All the ends of the earth shall remember
>and turn to the Lᴏʀᴅ,
and all the families of the nations
>shall worship before you.
For kingship belongs to the Lᴏʀᴅ,
>and he rules over the nations.

All the prosperous of the earth eat and worship;
>before him shall bow all who go down to the dust,
>even the one who could not keep himself alive.

Posterity shall serve him;
    it shall be told of the Lord to the coming generation;
they shall come and proclaim his righteousness to a people yet
       unborn,
    that he has done it.

—PSALM 22

For we must all appear before the judgment seat of Christ, so that each of us may receive what is due us for the things done while in the body, whether good or bad. **—2 CORINTHIANS 5:10 NIV**

PRAYER

God of love, God of mercy, God of justice, thank you for being a God who defends the afflicted and saves us from injustice. Thank you for being a righteous and holy and fair judge. Thank you for loving me, and thank you for giving us the opportunity to love others.

DAY 60

Social Justice Creed

Whoever acknowledges me before others, I will also acknowledge before my Father in heaven. —**MATTHEW 10:32 NIV**

MAKING A PUBLIC confession of faith is an important Christian tradition. Throughout Christian history, people who decided to make a serious commitment to following the life and teachings of Jesus would publicly declare their allegiance to Christ. This was done through the act of baptism and partaking in communion.

This often meant willingly putting themselves at risk of persecution, ranging from experiencing imprisonment to violence and even death. Until recently, in many places the expectation of entering the Christian faith was one of extreme sacrifice and hardship, where opposition was expected from society, governments, family, and friends. Now many countries have accepted Christianity as a mainstream faith, where it has even become the predominant religion, dominating the political, social, and even corporate segments of a nation. This has given its adherents many newfound societal privileges and advantages, such as the right to publicly worship, and widespread political support.

But these benefits have come at the cost of a few valuable concessions, and one of them is the mindset of Christianity as a sacrificial endeavor. Rather than costing us our lives and requiring heavy sacrifices, Christianity has now—for those of us in wealthier countries—become a modern cash cow, a way to gain fame, fortune, and power. In these environments it's easier to identify as a Christian than not to identify as one. Here Christianity has become so embedded within society that any request for the same freedoms and benefits as Christians is misinterpreted as a form of attack on the status quo, of being a type of persecution and threat to Christianity—even when it's not.

Social justice work within Christianity reaches back to its historical foundation as a sacrificial faith, a lifestyle that requires selflessness. Rather than seek power, it seeks to best love others, even at the cost of being alienated. It often requires abandoning the quest for comfort, fortune, and influence. Following the earliest Christian tradition of public baptisms and creeds, social justice requires a public declaration of solidarity with the oppressed. First, let's look at one of the very first Christian creeds, the Apostles' Creed, which is a basic summary of the Christian faith:

> I believe in God, the Father almighty,
>   creator of heaven and earth.

> I believe in Jesus Christ, his only Son, our Lord,
>   who was conceived by the Holy Spirit
>   and born of the virgin Mary.
>   He suffered under Pontius Pilate,
>   was crucified, died, and was buried;
>   he descended to hell.

The third day he rose again from the dead.
He ascended to heaven
and is seated at the right hand of God the Father almighty.
From there he will come to judge the living and the dead.

I believe in the Holy Spirit,
  the holy catholic* church,
  the communion of saints,
  the forgiveness of sins,
  the resurrection of the body,
  and the life everlasting. Amen.

*i.e., universal

Now, let's summarize social justice into a creed.

Social Justice Creed

Because we love Jesus and follow Christ's life and words, we believe in the Christian practice of social justice.

We believe in the full humanity and divine worth of all people, celebrating and accepting their race, ethnicity, culture, skin color, ability, gender, religion, belief, age, nationality, and identity. We love immigrants, refugees, the poor, the disabled, LGBTQIA+ individuals, BIPOC individuals, and everyone, even ourselves, and affirm that all are passionately loved by God and made in God's holy image.

We believe that any form of oppression, exploitation, prejudice, discrimination, and injustice is evil. It is our sacred duty to pursue justice, liberation, peace, mercy, and love for all of humanity. Amen.

Both the Apostles' Creed and the Social Justice Creed are public confessions of faith, and they don't contradict each other. The Apostles' Creed should naturally lead the Christian towards the Social Justice Creed. They go together, like Jesus and love, like Christianity and social justice work.

MEDITATION

Are you comfortable publicly declaring the Social Justice Creed? If you're uncomfortable doing so, why?

PRAYER

God of justice, God of love, and God of mercy, I love you. I commit to following the life and words of Jesus, and to loving you and my neighbors to the very best of my ability. With Jesus as my inspiration and ever-present strength, I dedicate my life to justice, mercy, and love.

Notes

1 James H. Cone, *The Cross and the Lynching Tree* (Maryknoll, NY: Orbis Books, 2011).

2 *Lexico Dictionaries*, s.v. "social justice," accessed May 6, 2021, https://www.lexico.com/en/definition/social_justice.

3 Merriam-Webster, s.v. "social justice," accessed May 6, 2021, https://www.merriam-webster.com/dictionary/social%20justice.

4 John Piper, "Hell Is Social Justice. We Need Social Mercy," Twitter, June 30, 2013, https://twitter.com/JohnPiper/status/351426102725578754.

5 Bryce Young, "Only Christians Understand True Social Justice," *Desiring God*, February 18, 2017, https://www.desiringgod.org/articles/only-christians-understand-true-social-justice.

6 Joe Carter is an editor for the Gospel Coalition. Joe Carter, "The FAQs: What Christians Should Know About Social Justice," *The Gospel Coalition*, August 17, 2018, https://www.thegospelcoalition.org/article/faqs-christians-know-social-justice/.

7 https://www.vatican.va/archive/ENG0015/_INDEX.HTM.

8 *Lexico Dictionaries*, s.v. "social," accessed May 6, 2021, https://www.lexico.com/en/definition/social.

9 *Lexico Dictionaries*, s.v. "justice," accessed May 6, 2021, https://www.lexico.com/en/definition/justice.

The Author

STEPHEN MATTSON is a writer and activist whose work has been published in *Relevant*, *Huffington Post*, *Sojourners*, Red Letter Christians, and a variety of other venues. Mattson graduated from Moody Bible Institute, served as a youth pastor, and now works at University of Northwestern—St. Paul. He and his wife and children live near Saint Paul, Minnesota. His first book, *The Great Reckoning: Surviving a Christianity That Looks Nothing Like Christ*, released in 2018.